A Passion
for Whisky

A Passion for Whisky

How the tiny Scottish island of Islay creates malts that captivate the world

Ian Wisniewski

Illustrated by Melvyn Evans

MITCHELL BEAZLEY

Contents

Introduction

A lamplit street led me from Bowmore distillery to a stone pier. It was a serene summer evening on Islay, the full moon casting a band of shimmering silver across the darkness of Loch Indaal; white and amber lights indicated the opposite shore. I raised a glass of Bowmore to toast this view, and took a sip: soft, creamy vanilla and wafting smoke enchanted my palate. Then I was no longer aware of flavours, or thoughts or even myself; just emotions creating an eternal moment. This is the magnificence of malt whisky: it transcends flavour and creates an experience.

I had arrived earlier that day, later than expected as the flight was delayed. But at least I was there. Sometimes the plane takes off from Glasgow airport, but then has to land there as well. Reaching Islay depends on the weather and visibility. The ferry from Kennacraig doesn't always reach Islay either, if the weather and sea don't cooperate. That's the time to repeat an Islay phrase, 'Och, it'll be fine', and to accept that the situation will work itself out, somehow. Residents of Islay, known as Ileachs (pronounced *Ee-la-hs*), also refer to things happening in 'Islay time', meaning don't worry, it will happen, just not right now. I'm a glutton for punctuality by nature, always arriving early, and I prefer spontaneity when it's planned. But when I embraced the Islay approach, it was liberating.

Ileachs have another endearing tradition. Drivers wave to each other as they pass by, not because they are all acquainted – the population of 3,200 makes that a fanciful notion. It's a courtesy known as the Islay wave, which entails raising a finger or two from the steering wheel, or the entire hand. If I drove on Islay I'd do the same. But having passed my driving test at the seventh attempt, I'm more qualified to be a passenger and free to savour the views from buses or taxis.

Much of Islay is flat or gently undulating, and peat bogs abound. It's a natural asset that endows Islay malts with smoky, earthy, peaty, medicinal and maritime notes. Such distinctive flavours create a sense of adventure and challenge, which explains why peated malts are considered an ultimate style of malt whisky.

I find peated malts exciting and deeply rewarding. I can be called a Smokehead, Peathead, Peatfreak. That's fine. I don't consider these terms pejorative; they simply confirm who I am. Similarly, when I'm called a whisky geek or nerd, I accept this as an acknowledgement that I cherish detail. Each detail is integral to the final result, and exploring detail is an illuminating and fulfilling way to live. Writing this book provided plenty of opportunities for me to explore detail, but it was never intended to be a production manual, a history book or a brand directory. I've focussed on certain details to evoke a sense of each distillery's individuality, together with some of the personalities who have shaped this, and the distillery managers who are the current custodians. And as the climate and topography of Islay play a formative role in the character of the malts, I also wanted to convey the character of the island.

I've included tasting notes for just a few selected expressions from each distillery, to indicate the house style and the range this encompasses. Some of these malts are currently available and some are 'archival' bottlings, which can be purchased from specialist dealers and auctions.

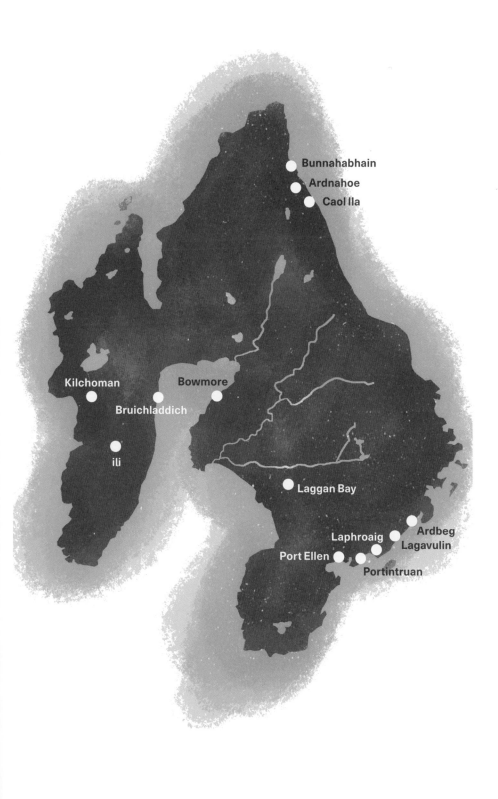

Bunnahabhain

Ardnahoe

Caol Ila

Kilchoman

Bowmore

Bruichladdich

ili

Laggan Bay

Ardbeg

Laphroaig

Lagavulin

Port Ellen

Portintruan

Chapter One

The irresistible rise of Islay malts

Chapter One

The irresistible rise of Islay malts

Rather than trying to condense the history of distilling on Islay into a few thousand words, I'd like to focus on recent history, since the past 50 years have (arguably) been the most decisive. But first, some context.

The earliest written reference to malt whisky dates from 1494, an entry in Scotland's Exchequer Rolls, or tax records. This indicates that malt whisky had already been distilled for some time on the mainland, and distillation is thought to have begun on Islay in the sixteenth century.

Malt whisky was the original and only style of Scotch whisky for centuries, until blended Scotch (a recipe of malt and grain whisky) emerged in the mid-nineteenth century. The objective was for blends to be a mellower, more 'approachable' style compared to rich, robust malts. It worked. Blends took off, and malt whisky was relegated to being a component of blends, which also meant that malt's future prospects depended on sales of blended Scotch. Sales increased and then decreased on a regular basis. Growth during the 1960s, for example, slowed down in the late 1970s and dwindled in the early 1980s. This resulted in a number of distilleries moving from full-time to part-time production, or closing. Another consequence was a growing stock of malt and grain whiskies with nothing to do except remain in their casks and continue ageing. Admittedly, some malt whisky was being sold by independent bottlers (rather than distilleries), on an ad hoc rather than continuous basis. But the quantities were tiny and the customers were a small, select group: the gentry and connoisseurs. Bowmore and Laphroaig had a following, and a few pioneering distilleries including Glenfiddich and The Glenlivet began to promote their malts more actively, which attracted interest among metropolitan bohemians. And then there was a major development in 1989, when the Classic Malts launched. This was a set of six single malts from different regions, comprising Lagavulin, Glenkinchie, Talisker, Dalwhinnie, Oban and Cragganmore, marketed collectively by the proprietor United Distillers (now part of Diageo) to showcase the styles and flavours malt whisky offered. The set of six was displayed as an ensemble on a specially designed pedestal in retail outlets and on bar counters. The Classic Malts were also available as a set of miniatures, which was an ideal way to explore the category.

Growing interest in single malts during the 1990s increased the number and range of releases, with Bowmore and Laphroaig the most active Islay malts. Interest was based on regionality as much as individual distilleries. Each region – the Highlands (including Speyside), Lowlands, Islay and Campbeltown – was assigned a stylistic definition that made it easier to navigate the category. These were (inevitably) generalizations, as each distillery is, of course, free to choose its own house style. Islay malts were defined as heavily peated, but the reality has long been a comprehensive range from unpeated through to light, medium and heavily peated.

An opportunity to experience some elite Islay malts was made possible by the Rare Malts series, an annual release of limited-edition malts owned by Diageo, that ran from 1995 to 2005. Caol Ila first appeared in the line-up in 1996 with a 20 year old malt distilled in 1975, then again in 1997 and 1998, when the first Port Ellen also featured: a 20 year old distilled in 1978. Diageo launched a similar programme under the Special Releases banner in 2001. The inaugural year included a Port Ellen 22 year old distilled in 1978, and two expressions of Talisker. These received such applause that between 2002 and 2005, several bottlings of Port Ellen, Lagavulin and Caol Ila were launched.

Meanwhile, Ardbeg reopened in 1997 and Bruichladdich reopened in 2001. Additionally, Caol Ila launched three continually available expressions in 2002. However, independent bottlers still provided the broadest range of Islay malts during the 1990s and 2000s.

'As independent bottlers often purchased stock from distilleries in batches, these were typically ad hoc, single-cask bottlings, and usually less expensive than proprietary bottlings. But that began to change from the 2010s onwards, and prices of independently bottled whisky can now be the same (or sometimes even higher), depending on the reputation of the independent bottler,' says Isabel Graham-Yooll, Director of Whisky.Auction, an online platform for buying and selling Scotch whisky and other spirits.

Malt whisky continued to account for a minority of Scotch whisky sales, which were still dominated by blended Scotch. But blends weren't creating any excitement, while malts were creating plenty, and Islay was at the forefront. Islay excitement had an inevitable focus – the peating level – and 'the higher the better' was a typical refrain. This preference also reflected a broader change in taste, with a move away from tea to coffee, and from white wine to bigger, richer red wines.

An ideal way of experiencing Islay malts, and discovering the island, was to attend Fèis Ìle (The Islay Festival). This originated in 1986 as a celebration of Islay culture, music, drama and storytelling, with the first whisky tasting added to the programme in 1990. Islay's distilleries became more involved from the year 2000, and when I attended my first Fèis Ìle in 2006, each distillery held an open day during the festival. This included a distillery tour, of course, as well as talks and tastings, while evening events included ceilidhs (social dances). I love dancing and always joined in, though I'm freestyle rather than any particular genre. I had no idea how to do the traditional teapot or strip-the-willow moves, but no one minded incorrect footwork or arm movements. All that mattered was enthusiasm, and I had plenty of that.

During Fèis Ìle the island's population is local, national and international. I met people from Islay, other Scottish islands, the Scottish mainland, Germany, Scandinavia, the USA and Japan. It's very easy to begin a conversation, as everyone is present for the same reason.

Appreciation of Islay malts continued to grow, including a new demographic of people in their late twenties and thirties, which was traditionally considered young for a malt whisky drinker. Another long-standing belief was that anyone's first step into Scotch whisky would be blended Scotch, followed by an excursion into elegant, fruity malts, which might subsequently extend into peated malts. But this was made redundant, as more people bypassed blends and fruity malts, and went straight to peated malts. And why not? No one needs to start with poached fish before moving on to sautéed and then the barbecued version. It's all about the flavours we enjoy.

Innovation at Islay's distilleries resulted in a greater range and level of expressions being released. A greater appreciation of varied peating levels followed, rather than focussing on the highest. Islay malts were also thriving on the secondary or resale market, meaning discontinued expressions and limited editions that had sold out in the primary retail market, such as whisky shops.

The secondary market originated in the 1990s when some specialist retailers, such as Milroy's in London, began to offer malts no longer in production. A growing number of collectors also resulted in specialist retailers, dealers and auction houses becoming more active in the secondary market. Islay malts were a major target for collectors, and growing demand for finite bottlings saw prices grow. 'Generally interest in Islay whisky is all-encompassing. It can be easy to fall into the trap of conflating auction prices with the level of interest, but just because certain distilleries cost bidders less does not mean they are in less demand,' says Joe Wilson, head of auction content at online platform Whisky Auctioneer.

Collectors are teased, even derided for buying malt whisky and consigning it to a display cabinet rather than opening and enjoying it. But for a collector, enjoyment stems from possessing: opening the bottle is impossible, as it would no longer be in perfect original condition. I'm a collector. But as a whisky lover I also want to taste the whisky. It's a dilemma. Some limited-edition releases offered a solution to this by including a miniature, for tasting, together with the full-sized bottle that could remain intact. But collectors couldn't resist collecting the accompanying miniature. While miniatures and full-sized bottles have equal stature for me, miniatures are, of course, far easier to accommodate though don't always have a mini-price.

'Some miniatures are still affordable, whereas the equivalent full-sized bottle isn't,' advises Isabel Graham-Yooll, 'though a mini can also be rarer than the equivalent full-sized bottle, and so more expensive. Miniatures were part of our auctions from the start, though we've held dedicated auctions of miniatures every three months since November 2017. We now expect new record prices to be set at each auction of miniatures.'

For non-collectors, miniatures can play a very different role. 'People will also buy miniatures as a means of sampling whiskies without having to commit to a full bottle,' says Joe Wilson. 'Those wanting to try the older 1980s Laphroaig 10, Lagavulin 12 or Ardbeg Guaranteed 10 year old, for example, may find more joy bidding on miniatures than wading into the competitive market for the full-size versions.'

Regular auctions, with results available online, provide continual updates on prices achieved for Islay malts. I can check the latest price paid for a bottle I have, or see how much I'd have to pay for a desired addition to my collection. However, the latest auction price is not a guarantee of the value.

'When a so-called legendary bottle comes to auction for the first time in a long time, you will see highly competitive bidding that pushes the price into record-breaking territory. Should another example of the bottle come to auction again too soon, the bidder willing to pay the highest price last time already has one, so it is not uncommon to expect the price to be slightly lower,' continues Joe.

Purchasers used to be either collectors (who divided into those collecting miniatures or full-sized bottles) or connoisseurs who were drinkers. And once it was clear how rapidly and significantly prices were increasing, investors also bought into the category.

'The price point at which a bottle is bought to drink or to collect or to keep as an investment varies enormously. I would expect that there are people successfully bidding with all three motivations and at every level of pricing,' says Joe. 'For every Bowmore 1966 Samaroli Bouquet that is hailed as a groundbreaking investment bottle, there are speculators looking at more modern releases trying to get the next groundbreaking investment. Equally, there are those who want to try whiskies hailed as being historically significant.'

Islay's distillery managers, master distillers and master blenders were increasingly in demand at whisky festivals from the 1990s, and particularly since the millennium, and ever more revered by a growing global fan club. A huge increase in the number of whisky festivals around Europe, Scandinavia, Asia and North America meant that travelling and presenting could easily be a full-time job. And with more people travelling to Islay, facilities were continually being added and extended, with Kilchoman and Ardnahoe, for example, opening new visitor centres in 2020. But they soon had to close. The Covid-19 pandemic led to lockdown being announced in the UK in March 2020. Non-essential travel was not allowed, which meant no tourists arriving and no Ileachs leaving the island. The Islay Resilience Group, an amalgamation of community groups, ensured that everyone on the island remained connected. Distilleries stopped producing for varying lengths of time, from several weeks to a few months.

Meanwhile, with so many people largely confined to their homes, distilleries experienced greatly increased sales online, and maintained contact with the locked-down world through online tastings. Fèis Île could only be a virtual event in 2020 and 2021, returning to an in-person festival in 2022.

When I visited Islay to research this book in December 2022 and January 2023, there were nine operational distilleries and four more on the way – which means we already have a lot to enjoy, and soon there will be even more.

Ingredients, climate & the production process

Chapter Two

Ingredients, climate & the production process

Islay provides fertile land to grow barley, but farmers have to contend with various challenges before they can gather the harvest. The climate can cooperate or complicate. Islay's mild temperatures and sunshine, for example, are advantageous. But up to 200 days of rainfall annually, and winds exceeding 12 miles per hour from various directions, are definitely not.

Historically, Islay distilleries were attached to a farm that supplied barley, though importing barley from the mainland has long been standard practice. This essentially means from Aberdeenshire, the Black Isle and Dundee, and on to the Borders, since the east of Scotland is significantly drier and sunnier than Islay. However, in 2004 barley was cultivated on Islay for distilling, the first time in living memory. Commissioned by Bruichladdich, the distillery's Islay barley project evolved to include 19 farmers across the island, enabling 45 per cent of production in 2020 to be locally grown. Barley from selected farms is stored separately, designated to be made into a single-farm-origin malt, while barley from other farms is combined and spread across all three of the distillery's expressions: Bruichladdich, Port Charlotte and Octomore.

Similarly, Kilchoman has been distilling Islay barley, which is grown in fields surrounding the distillery, since 2005. 'We're increasing the amount of barley we are growing,' says Anthony Wills, founder of Kilchoman. 'The farm has potentially 430 acres that we can cultivate, though this needs to be on a rotational basis. Currently we're at 130 acres, and will go up to 200 acres by 2023. This will provide 400 tonnes of barley, representing 20–25 per cent of our total needs.'

Malt whisky is distilled from varieties of spring barley, which is sown from early April because the temperature needs to be above 10°C (50°F), and the moisture level of the soil needs to be below 20–22 per cent. If the moisture level is higher (which is perfectly possible with Islay's rainfall), farmers must decide whether to risk it and sow, or to take a different risk, and wait (and hope) for the moisture level to decrease. Nature, of course, doesn't provide any guarantees. This also applies to the greylag geese that spend the winter on Islay, and which used to fly to Greenland and Iceland at the end of March in order to breed. But this schedule began to change around 2015. Now, some but not all fly off in early to mid-April (whether this is due to changing weather patterns is uncertain). For farmers, it's preferable that all geese depart on time.

'Some greylag geese now breed here on Islay, and hundreds can land together on a field sown with barley, pecking at the ground to eat the seeds,' says James Brown, who owns Octomore Farm (where the Octomore distillery once stood) by Port Charlotte. 'Rooks also fly down from trees in the village and eat the barley. Scarecrows don't make any difference. There's no point being stressed; you just have to accept it and hope for the best. They can't eat all the seeds.'

Sowing one acre takes James about 20 minutes, and with mild rainfall and warm temperatures, the first shoots appear in about three weeks. Sunshine is required in late June when barley flowers for a week or so, which helps to set the seeds. Spring barley is 'two row', which means rows of two seeds side by side, with about 24–30 seeds per head. Barley attains its full height in early August when the ear appears. Approaching harvest, the ideal conditions are more sunshine and less rain.

'The best harvest recently was 2021. A lot of it is luck, good weather, machines not breaking down. If I get 2 tonnes of barley per acre I'm delighted,' says James. This is significantly less than mainland yields, which are typically 5–6 tonnes per acre, but then Islay's climate is significantly less favourable. Whether yields on Islay improve remains to be seen, as plant breeders continually develop new barley varieties that offer greater susceptibility to disease, higher yields per hectare for the farmer and higher yields of alcohol per tonne for the distiller.

For example, in mainland Scotland, Optic was the number one barley variety between 2000 and 2011, yielding around 5.3 tonnes per hectare and 410 litres (90 gallons) of alcohol per tonne. Concerto took over from 2012–18, yielding around 5.7 tonnes per hectare, and 412 litres (91 gallons) per tonne. In 2018, Laureate offered 6 tonnes per hectare and 414 litres (91.1 gallons) per tonne.

New varieties are submitted for approval by the Malting Barley Committee at the Institute of Brewing & Distilling. The first stage is gaining Provisional Approval 1. If test results continue successfully, then Provisional Approval 2 or even Full Approval can be gained the following year. Various Islay distilleries are using Laureate and KWS Sassy, which both gained full approval in 2017. Laureate has a short straw (i.e. height), making it better able to withstand high winds and, together with KWS Sassy, also offers very high resistance to mildew. Another consideration is whether individual barley varieties yield new make spirit with discernible differences. 'We were distilling Concerto until 2022, with Sassy replacing it in 2023. Sassy produced new make spirit with a richer, creamier character,' says Anthony Wills at Kilchoman.

Islay's particular peat

Sightseeing on Islay doesn't require a special excursion; there are memorable sights wherever you go. The road from Port Ellen to Bowmore, for example, passes through a broad expanse of flat land, the turf tinged with tufts of caramel and sienna. Just beneath this surface layer is an underworld of deep, dark, glistening peat, the result of vegetation that has gradually decomposed and became compressed, as layer upon layer built up over 10,000–18,000 years.

Islay peat contains deluxe levels of different mosses, of which sphagnum is the most prominent and the most instrumental, together with grasses, bog myrtle, heather and significant levels of seaweed. Sand is also a component – historic ocean sand washed up when Islay was formed – and contributes saltiness to the peat. Salt levels peak in coastal peat, whereas Islay's inland and hillside peat is more fibrous, due to higher levels of bog myrtle and heather. However, regular rainfall adds sea spray wherever it falls, and the most plentiful component of peat is water, accounting for up to 75 per cent. The level of water depends on the amount of sphagnum moss, which varies among peat bogs. This moss has small branches and leaves that are able to retain many times their own body weight in water, even after they stop living. The level of water determines the rate at which vegetation decays, which is more gradual in wetter bogs.

The peat-cutting season is April to September, when peat bogs are (hopefully) dry enough to walk upon. Islay peat is either cut by hand or mechanically involving tractors. Learning how to cut by hand takes time. Derek Scott, who provides Kilchoman with peat, spent a year alongside an experienced peat cutter. Derek's peat bank is 180 metres (200 yards) from the shores of Loch Gorm, Islay's largest freshwater loch, home to numerous brown trout and a small island with the ruins of an eighteenth-century castle. 'Working between April and July I hear tremendous birdsong; there are skylarks, curlews, herons and geese around me, and it's not unusual to see an osprey eating a fish in the loch, though adders can be a problem,' says Derek.

The first step is marking a trench 65 metres (213 feet) long, from which peat is extracted using a peat cutter (or peat spade). The handle is traditionally made from a redundant cask stave, with a long wooden pole that has an additional protruding blade like a fin on one side of the tip. The length of the peat cutter, which is around 60 cm (24 in) long and 15 cm (6 in) wide, determines the dimensions of the peat slab extracted. The top layer of turf is removed and set aside; once the trench has been excavated, the turf is replaced to form a surface that regenerates. Three underlying layers of peat are extracted, one layer at a time. The top layer is the most fibrous, and the spade is sharpened regularly with a file so that it can cut through the roots of bog myrtle. The second layer is much darker and oilier, and the third layer is the darkest, being the oldest. Every 2–3 cm (1 in) represents 1,000 years of decomposition.

'You're cutting beneath your feet and this angle makes it really difficult work, so 3 to 4 hours at a time is as much as I can do,' Derek continues. 'Locals often come over for a chat when they see me cutting, older chaps usually, who 40–50 years ago were cutting peat to heat their homes. And when guys stop to chat they often help out too and show me how they do it, as everyone has their own style and their advice is very welcome.'

When freshly cut, peat can be removed in one piece, despite a moisture level of around 80 per cent, which includes plenty of oil leaking out. The peat needs to dry and this happens on location, laying pieces flat on the ground. Within a few weeks of dry, windy weather, the surface of the peat forms a skin that is waterproof. Each piece is then turned over to expose and dry the other side. In 3 to 4 weeks the moisture level usually reaches around 7–8 per cent, which also sees each piece shrink by around one-third. Pieces of peat can then be handled and stacked for further drying, either in a criss-cross pattern forming a small tower, or leaning upright against each other like a tipi.

Machine-cut peat is harvested using a tractor customized with three vast, wide wheels on either side to prevent it from sinking into the peat (tractors have been lost in this way). The tractor pulls a harvester attachment fitted with a circular saw or a chainsaw. This creates a trench several centimetres (a couple of inches) wide, while the depth can be adjusted to cut from 0.5–2 metres (1½–6½ feet), so extraction can be much shallower than hand cutting. Different machines have individual methods of extruding peat. It can be compressed within a chamber in the harvester, prior to being deposited as evenly spaced 'bricks' of peat, around 10 cm (4in) square, on the ground behind the machine as it continues along the trench. These bricks dry where they fall, and are collected around a month later. Alternatively, peat can be squeezed out of a tube within the machine like a very long sausage, for the entire length of the trench. A harvester can cut several trenches and produce a peat sausage from each trench simultaneously. A skin forms on the surface of the peat as it begins to dry, usually within 3 to 4 hours, which prevents rain being absorbed. As the peat continues to dry over the next few weeks, natural shrinkage breaks it up into manageable lengths of around 10–40 cm (4–16in), with a diameter of 5–10 cm (2–4in).

Islay peat is certainly distinctive, being lightly oily, with iodine, medicinal, salty and even tarry notes. This differs from peat in other Scottish regions such as Speyside, which contains plenty of Scotch pine, heather and sphagnum moss (and lacks maritime influence). However, the extent to which components within the peat influence the character of a malt whisky is uncertain, as research has not established direct links.

The use of peat also raises the question of sustainability, and ensuring that a natural asset can be regenerated rather than reduced. In Scotland overall, 1 per cent of peat extracted is used by the malt whisky industry, and research into maximizing the influence of peat while reducing the amount used is ongoing. Moreover, regeneration is an integral part of cutting peat. 'I only cut as much as peat as is needed, and replace the turf to make it look as though I haven't been there,' says Derek.

Malting

Malting is the traditional process used to make barley germinate, which is a preliminary stage that subsequently enables the barley to be distilled. Traditionally, each distillery had floor maltings where this was conducted. Being entirely manual, the process requires significant experience, and the volume of barley that can be malted is limited by the size of the floors, not to mention a 7 to 10-day schedule for each batch. Many distilleries closed their floor maltings in the 1960s, when growing demand for Scotch whisky led to increased production and floor maltings could not keep up. Instead, orders were placed with commercial maltings, which operate on a greater scale and shorter time frame, using automated vessels that can also peat the barley to various levels. Only a few of Scotland's approximately 130 malt whisky distilleries continue to operate floor maltings; these include Ardnamurchan and Glen Garioch in the Highlands, The Balvenie and Benriach in Speyside, Springbank in Campbeltown and Highland Park on Orkney. This makes it even more amazing that three Islay distilleries operate floor maltings: Bowmore, Kilchoman and Laphroaig. Bruichladdich is additionally planning to open floor maltings.

Steeping

The first stage of the malting process is steeping, which takes place in steeps, traditionally large stone or cast iron troughs, with stainless steel the more contemporary option. Water is added to the steeps, which the grain takes up through the micropyle (small opening) at its tip. This is the only entry point for water, as the outer layers of the grain are waterproof. The moisture level of the barley increases from 12 per cent to around 30 per cent over the next eight to ten hours. The remaining water is then drained from the steep, and the barley receives an 'air rest' for around eight hours. This dispels carbon dioxide, a natural by-product of the process, and enables the barley to take in oxygen from the air, which increases its energy levels and enables a more rapid uptake of water.

A second batch of fresh water is then added, raising the barley's moisture level to around 40 per cent after eight hours, at which point the water is drained and another air rest follows. At this stage, a small white root tip, known as a chit, appears at one end of the grain. A third and final batch of water is added and drained after eight hours, followed by an air rest. The barley then has a moisture level of up to 45 per cent, and the root tip has grown into a rootlet about the same length as the grain itself.

The barley is removed from the steeps and spread across a stone or concrete malting floor in order to germinate over four to five days. During this time, the bed of barley is regularly 'turned' to bring underlying barley to the surface. This is done using a wooden shovel called a malt shiel, to dig and redistribute barley across the surface. A plough (a scaled-down wooden version of a farmer's plough) pulled by a malt man is another way of doing this.

Turning is essential because germination naturally produces heat, up to 20–22°C (68–72°F), with the temperature of underlying barley significantly higher than on the surface. Higher temperatures promote faster rates of germination, so turning ensures that all the barley experiences the same conditions, and germinates at the same rate.

Germination instigates significant changes within the grain. Various enzymes are activated, the most significant being alpha amylase, beta amylase and limit dextrinase. (Enzymes subsequently play a vital role during the mashing process by converting starches into sugars.)

Each grain contains numerous 'packets' of starch incarcerated within cell walls. These walls are broken down during germination, which enables the embryo to access starch as a food source to generate energy for growth. This is when any further growth is prevented by drying the barley using the heat of kilning. Otherwise, the embryo would use up starch to grow, leaving less starch from which to produce alcohol.

A traditional test to check that the barley is ready for kilning is to split a grain open with a fingernail and rub the contents between the finger and thumb. If this produces a smooth paste (starch), the crucial development has occurred. A lack of white powder indicates that the starch is still enclosed within cell walls, and requires longer to germinate. Another traditional test was chewing the malt; if the texture resembled soft banana, and it tasted like yeasty, starchy dough, it was ready. Yet another option was for the malt man (who oversaw the process) to inscribe his initials on a spade using a grain. If they were legible, the malt was ready.

Smoke and heat

Barley has a moisture level of around 45 per cent at the start of kilning, and is spread out on a perforated floor above a kiln to form a 'bed'. If the malt is intended for unpeated production, it is dried using hot air, which reduces the moisture level to around 4.5–5 per cent. The heat of kilning also develops the flavour of the barley, converting the starchy, grainy character into sweet, malty, digestive biscuit notes.

If the malt is being peated, a fire is started in the kiln using wood, and peat is added to produce smoke. This rises up, passing through the perforated floor, and is absorbed by the barley, essentially the husk, though the interior of the grain also absorbs a modest amount. Peating typically takes 16–24 hours. Adding smaller amounts of peat to the kiln over a shorter period produces lower levels of peating. Using more peat for longer creates higher peating levels. This may sound like a straightforward formula, but skill and experience are required to create a consistent level of 'peat reek' (peat smoke), while preventing flames from breaking through. Phenolic compounds within the peat, which convey the peaty, smoky characteristics to the barley, can be destroyed by flames. Similarly, achieving specific peating levels relies entirely on the experience of the operator, without the benefit of gauges or display screens. The kiln only offers one low-tech option: opening or closing the doors to increase or reduce air flow. Increased air flow helps to draw the fire and raise the heat.

The top layers of peat are more fibrous, creating more smoke than other cuts of peat but less heat, which entails the risk of the fire dwindling. (Restarting the fire is not an option, as it would require raking out the existing fire, which would take long enough to seriously compromise the batch of malt.) Underlying layers of peat are oilier and contain more carbon, which produces more heat but less smoke.

Another control mechanism is selecting peat on the basis of the moisture levels, which range from around 10–45 per cent. Very dry peat produces heat but little smoke, and so a lower level of phenolics. However, adding caff, small pieces of dry peat less than 5 cm (2in) in diameter, can plug any gaps, which impedes air flow and produces more smoke. Dry peat can also be hosed with water (which it holds well) to help cool the fire if it is getting rampant, as it burns less intensely and produces more smoke. Consequently, the kiln operator assembles a range of drier and wetter peat as well as different layers and sizes of peat to control the fire.

During peating, the bed is 'turned' to ensure all the grains experience the same conditions, otherwise the base of the bed could easily be oversmoked and the surface undersmoked. Traditionally, operators turned the bed using a rake or shovel, though the level of smoke in the air meant health and safety regulations stopped this practice. The solution was fitting mechanical turners: a bar fitted with rotating 'paddles' moves back and forth across the floor, using runners on rails attached to the walls of the kiln.

There is a deadline by which the peating level must be achieved, as smoke is absorbed by the barley while it retains moisture on the surface. Once moisture is driven from the surface of the barley, kilning reaches the 'break point' around 38°C (100°F), when heat begins to draw moisture from within the grain. Temperature is important, as the enzymes contained within the barley are heat-sensitive when the grain is wet, but less likely to be damaged by heat once the grain is drier (after the break point). The temperature can then be increased to around 78°C (172°F) to dry the malt using hot air for around 25–40 hours in order to reduce the moisture level to 4.5–5 per cent.

Peated malt
The result of peating is typically described as smoky, peaty notes, though the levels of each vary significantly. Smoke ranges from gentle wafts to a bonfire on the beach. Peat includes earthy notes, heather, toasted and

charred wood, and embers. But there's far more on offer. This includes seaweed, sea spray and umami characteristics such as Parmesan, black olives in brine, chargrilled and barbecued notes. Another group comprises coal, tar, creosote and freshly laid asphalt, as well as medicinal notes such as carbolic soap and antiseptic.

These flavours stem from eight groups of phenolic compounds that are used as the traditional measure of peating levels. The compound present in the greatest quantity, accounting for up to 50 per cent of the total, is phenol (an individual group, whereas phenolic is an overall term that includes all groups). Cresol is usually around 40 per cent of the total, and guaiacol 10 per cent. These percentages vary, depending on the source and composition of the peat. But the percentages don't indicate how influential the compounds are. Phenol, for example, has the numbers but is the simplest compound: being quite shy, it only adds mellow medicinal aromas. Cresol is more assertive and complex, containing three subsidiary groups that can each deliver their own line-up of earthy, medicinal, tar and asphalt notes. Guaiacol is the most complex and most aroma-active phenolic compound, releasing smoky and medicinal notes. The overlap between guaiacol and cresol boosts the level of medicinal notes. Whether other synergies exist between phenolic compounds and the influence they may have is still being researched.

However, these characteristics are only evident when a compound is present at higher levels. At lower levels, phenolics have a more generic peaty, smoky character. There is no specific level at which such change occurs, as this depends on the other flavours present, and the sensitivity of whoever is assessing the malts, as levels of sensitivity (and insensitivity) to phenolics vary enormously.

The traditional way of expressing the peating level is in terms of ppm (parts per million). This is always an overall total, which doesn't specify levels of individual compounds. A level of 1 ppm is equivalent to 1 milligram in a litre. The lowest level at which phenolics are generally discernible in malt whisky is 2 ppm. Between 5 and 10 ppm is considered lightly peated, adding gentle wafts of smoke. Around 20–25 ppm is a medium level, with more distinct smoke, earthy, peaty, toasted and grilled notes, while 40–50 ppm and above is considered heavily peated, with billowing bonfire smoke, chargrilled, barbecued notes and robust, earthy peatiness.

The peating level is inevitably a focal point. However, this refers to the original peating level of the barley, which decreases during the production process, and can be 25–30 per cent lower in new make spirit. Moreover, the peating level is also no indication of the phenolic characteristics that make it into the new make spirit. Each phenolic compound contains a range of lighter and richer notes, and distillation enables desired phenolics to be retained, and others excluded. The role phenolics play in the new make spirit also depends on the house style, with a more elegant spirit showing the phenolics more clearly than a richer, bolder example.

Islay peat has a specific range of components, but the extent to which these contribute particular flavours is still being researched. This question is further complicated by the fact that peat smoke also contains many other flavour compounds (not phenolics) that are still being categorized. Whether and to what extent these other compounds may contribute flavour is currently uncertain. The technology that could provide an answer is not yet available.

Peated (as well as unpeated) malt can also gain additional flavours through the process of roasting. This is effectively an extreme version of kilning, which subjects the malt to temperatures of 200°C (392°F) or higher in a roasting drum. Applying such heat develops the flavour of the malt, initially adding nuttiness, then chocolate, coffee and mocha, while the malt retains the original digestive biscuit character. Roasting has only recently begun to be explored, with one prime example from Islay being Ardbeg Ardcore, released in 2022, which shows charcoal, sweet smoke, aniseed and dark chocolate, along with toffee notes.

Port Ellen Maltings

Islay distilleries place orders for malted barley with various commercial maltsters on the mainland, though a local source is Port Ellen Maltings in the town of Port Ellen. This was built in 1972 by Scottish Malt Distillers, a company then owned by three Islay distilleries: Port Ellen, Caol Ila and Lagavulin. These distilleries had decided that closing their floor maltings and being supplied by a single modern facility was more economical. However, the early 1980s downturn in the whisky industry saw Caol Ila and Lagavulin reduce production levels to well below capacity, and Port Ellen distillery closed in 1983. Consequently, far less malt was required, which made Port Ellen Maltings economically unviable. Closure seemed inevitable.

Fortunately, other Islay distilleries united to save the maltings by signing the Concordat of Islay Distillers in 1987. Every Islay distillery that was then operational – Ardbeg, Bunnahabhain, Bowmore, Bruichladdich, Caol Ila, Lagavulin and Laphroaig – together with the Isle of Jura distillery on neighbouring Jura pledged to take at least a percentage of its malt from Port Ellen Maltings. As these distilleries used a range of peating levels, from very light through to mild, medium, heavy and very heavy, providing such an à la carte service was very different from the maltings' original role of producing the same highly peated malt for three distilleries.

A ferry from Kennacraig brings barley to Port Ellen's sheltered deep-water harbour on Loch Leodamais. Water from Leorin Loch in the nearby hills fills the steeps. The germination drums, produced by the renowned firm of Robert Boby, are the largest in the UK. Each of the seven steel drums holds the contents of two steeps (50 tonnes of barley at original weight, 65 tonnes after steeping). Technically green malt at this stage, it is loaded into each drum through a chute at either end.

A perforated steel floor enables controlled volumes of air, generated by large fans, to be blown through the grain. This maintains the appropriate temperature, and the air is humidified with freshwater to promote the right humidity for growth. Circulating air also removes heat and carbon dioxide from the drum through vents. Continued growth sees the grains beginning to break down the cell walls in order to access the starch. After five days the cell walls have been broken down and the shoot extends for three-quarters of the grain's spine. Once released from the drums through four doors, resembling escape hatches, a large chute and conveyor belt transport the malt to the kiln.

The kilns operate in pairs. One conducts hot air to the malt and another is used to burn peat as required. Once peating is concluded, the malt is dried for around 25 hours or longer, the temperature rising from around 40–50°C (104–122°F) to 80°C (176°F), which reduces the moisture level to around 4.5–5 per cent. From the kiln, malt is fed to a dresser that detaches the rootlets. Combined with water and barley dust from storage vessels, the rootlets are shaped into pellets. Technically 'malt residuals,' and non-technically cattle feed, Islay's cows have a good appetite for these peaty pellets, but their counterparts on the mainland do not. Consequently, pellets for mainland cows are sweetened with molasses.

Crafting malt whisky

Every distillery follows the same process but does it differently, since each stage of production entails choices that influence the resulting new make spirit, and subsequently the malt whisky. Whether each influence is major or minor, they all add up to create an individual 'house style': elegantly fruity or richer and fuller-bodied, as well as unpeated or peated to various levels. Changing any detail can in turn alter this profile subtly or significantly.

Research has greatly increased understanding of the production process, but many questions remain unanswered. But do we really want everything to be explained? I do and I don't. I love learning, and will always be an eager student yearning for more knowledge. Yet I also enjoy malt whisky's mystique and the sense of alchemy. I remember at school deliberately not listening to a geography lesson that explained cumulonimbus clouds, as I preferred to marvel rather than understand them. Understanding all the options is, of course, paramount when reviewing production in an established distillery, or deciding on a production regime for a new distillery. And for anyone planning to open a new distillery on Islay, expert guidance for every stage of the process is readily available.

'We can design and build a distillery from start to finish, and have a library of designs to choose from, a quadrangle or circular design for example, and these layouts can be tailored to individual requirements and preferences. It takes at least two years from start to finish; three years is quite common,' says Richard Forsyth, chairman of Forsyths, a Scottish company that deals with every aspect of distilling.

Commissioning and manufacturing equipment can mean a lead time of 12–18 months, but in order to do this the production capacity must be decided. Richard continues: 'Let's say the production capacity is 1 million litres per year; this enables us to size up the mash tun, then work out the amount of fermenters needed, and the size of the pot still. The ideal set-up is that one mash tun can supply wort for one washback, which goes into one wash still and is then redistilled in one spirit still.'

The production regime can then be tailored to produce the desired house style. 'You can influence the new make spirit character to a certain extent, choosing the barley, yeast strain, fermentation times and spirit cut. But it's not an exact science, and some fine-tuning is always needed once production begins.'

These are all, of course, universal factors that apply wherever the location. But Islay entails extras, as Richard further explains: 'The costs of building on an island are at least 25 per cent more, and planning is even more vital. We prefabricate as much as possible in the workshop using the latest design systems, which gives a better-quality result. Precast concrete panels, for example, can be prepared on the mainland and shipped to construct ageing warehouses.'

Shipping means a lorry, and a ferry to ship the lorry. But with a growing number of distilleries relying upon a limited ferry service to deliver yeast, casks, spare parts and so on, the infrastructure is increasingly stretched and advance booking is essential. 'The size of the ferry is another limitation to consider; if necessary, mash tuns can be sent in two halves and assembled on Islay,' says Richard. 'Though we've managed to get entire pot stills onto the ferry.'

Each section of a distillery has its own characteristics. Seeing the malt mill is all about colour, usually either red or green, depending on the manufacturer, and hearing a rhythmic sound that ranges from a sewing machine to drumbeats. The mash house (in which mashing takes place) is noticeably warmer, with a background hum of running water, and aromas of creamy porridge. Silence amid the washbacks (fermentation vessels) belies the intense activity of fermentation, which is articulated by rich aromas – yeasty, cereal and fruit. The stillhouse (where distillation is conducted) radiates warmth from the stills, and the air can be fragrant with apples and pears.

Milling

The usual choice of malt mill is either a Porteus with a rich red livery, or a Robert Boby in deep green. Antique models continue to see active service on Islay, as these mills are so reliable that minimal maintenance is sufficient to keep them going. A mill is equipped with two pairs of rollers. The first pair cracks the husk and channels the malt into the second set of rollers for finer milling. Rollers are traditionally stone or wood, with stainless steel the more modern option. Each roller (in a pair) rotates in the opposite direction to its counterpart for more efficient milling.

The space between each pair of rollers is adjustable, and this determines the specification, or grade, to which the malt is milled. There are three grades of malt, with a typical ratio of 20 per cent husk, 70 per cent grits (or 'middles,' i.e. medium ground) and 10 per cent flour (or 'fines'). They are collectively known as the grist.

Mashing

The specification of the grist optimizes mashing, when starches are converted into sugars. Higher percentages of flour can increase the yield of sugars, but potentially turn the grist into a sticky porridge that complicates drainage. Higher percentages of husk improve drainage, but can also reduce the yield of sugars, so it's a case of balancing the options.

Grist and hot water meet above the mash tun and enter together through a spout. This first batch of water is invariably at 63.5°C (146°F), which enables two key enzymes, alpha amylase and beta amylase, to get to work. Both are sensitive to temperature. Alpha amylase prefers 70°C (158°F), but beta amylase likes it cooler, around 55°C (131°F), so the temperature of the first water is a compromise that doesn't alienate either enzyme. Hot water gelatinizes starches in the grits and fines, which enables the enzymes to get going. There's plenty to do, as the starches comprise extremely long chains of linked units, wrapped around each other in tight bundles like balls of wool.

Alpha amylase is effectively a random swinging axe hacking large starch bundles indiscriminately, which creates shorter, individual chains with a beginning and an end. Enter beta amylase, which has a very different approach, meticulously slicing off the last two units at the end of each chain, then the next two and so on, until it reaches the end. Then it's on to the next chain.

Some starch chains also have the equivalent of side shoots, which neither alpha nor beta amylase are able to deal with. But they have a colleague who can. Limit dextrinase strims these side shoots, enabling alpha amylase to start chopping, then beta amylase gets slicing. Such coordinated teamwork ensures that the wort (the sugary liquid that is the result of mashing) contains convenient, bite-sized sugars that yeast can metabolize (digest) during fermentation.

The husk doesn't contain starch, but has the greatest level of phenolics, which water rinses from the husk. Phenolics are also rinsed from grits and fines with the same ease, though the levels are far lower.

This sugary, phenolic water drains through perforated plates at the base of the mash tun.

A second addition of water, at a higher temperature of around 74°C (165°F), is sprayed onto the grist from a sparge ring, effectively a circular showerhead with nozzles positioned at the top of the mash tun. This second water repeats the work of the first water, creating more sugars and rinsing additional phenolics from the grist, before draining from the base of the mash tun.

Once the volume of wort needed for fermentation has drained, a third batch of water is added at 85°C (185°F) or higher. This extracts remaining sugars and rinses residual phenolics. The level of both is low but better than nothing, and this water, known as the sparge, is recycled as the first water of the next mashing cycle.

Mash tuns were traditionally cast iron, though stainless steel has been the norm since the 1980s, offering greater ease of cleaning. Mash tuns usually have a lid, copper or stainless steel, to maintain the water temperature within the mash tun. The grist, known as the bed, can get sticky during mashing, which slows drainage, so each mash tun has arms that rotate and can stir things up. The most historic type of arm is a rake, like a series of daddy longlegs spiders that rotates as the rake circulates the mash tun. In the 1970s, many rakes were replaced by semi-lauters, which have horizontal arms with 'fins' that rotate clockwise and anticlockwise. By the 1980s, this concept had evolved further into a lauter with arms that could also be raised or lowered, and so stir specific 'layers' of the bed. The principal benefit of semi-lauters and lauters was a reduction in the mashing time.

The degree of stirring varies among distilleries, as this has a profound influence on the resulting whisky. Minimal stirring produces clear wort; more stirring results in cloudy wort. Cloudiness is caused by small fragments of grist suspended in the liquid. As these fragments contain flavour compounds, cloudy wort promotes more cereal and nutty notes in the resulting spirit, and potentially a higher level of phenolics. The grist that remains in the mash tun, known as draff, retains a certain level of phenolics. This has a valuable role: it is served up to cows on the island and the mainland. Meanwhile, the wort advances to the next stage, when yeast is added to begin the fermentation process.

The significance of fermentation

Yeast has only one motivation during fermentation: to feast on sugars that provide the energy required to grow and reproduce. But this appetite is, inadvertently, responsible for a complex and transformative process. Metabolizing (digesting) sugars produces a residue that yeast cells emit from their systems into the surrounding liquid. This residue is alcohol and various flavour compounds, particularly esters, which span a range of fruit notes. The amount of yeast added to the wort is typically 2 per cent of the weight of malted barley. Using too little yeast risks decreasing the yield of alcohol and compromising the flavour profile. Too much yeast increases costs without any benefits.

Fermentation begins with the 'lag' phase, during which yeast acclimatizes to its new environment. Taking in oxygen present within the wort fuels initial growth and reproduction. Each yeast cell, which is elliptical and transparent, produces a small bud that grows. When it reaches half the size of the parent cell, the junior bud is liberated and continues growing. After reaching full size, the cell produces a small bud and the cycle begins again, producing the next generation.

Oxygen runs out after several hours, and this marks the beginning of the 'log' phase. The yeast turns to another source of energy: sugars and nutrients within the wort. First on the menu are glucose (comprising one molecule) and maltose (two linked molecules of glucose), being the simplest sugars and easiest to metabolize. These are something of an appetizer before yeast moves on to a more substantial course: maltotriose (three linked glucose molecules).

Dining on sugar is a process of absorption through a yeast cell's exterior membrane, and is undertaken by one particular organelle (a substructure within a cell that has an individual function), which also metabolizes the sugar and emits the resulting alcohol through the membrane. Each yeast cell contains various organelles, whose functions include absorbing nutrients from the wort, such as protein and fats, which are metabolized. The residue is a range of flavour compounds, emitted through the membrane into the wort. This log phase sees yeast grow and reproduce at the fastest rate, which also means increased production of alcohol and flavour compounds.

As fermentation continues, the supply of sugar dwindles, the temperature of the wort rises as a natural consequence of fermentation and the alcoholic strength of the wort increases, as does the level of acidity. Each individual factor stresses yeast cells, and collectively they cause mega-stress. The presence of phenolic compounds adds further anxiety; exactly why is uncertain, but is thought to be due to phenolics increasing the level of acidity in the wort. (Ironically, phenolics are also among the flavour compounds yeast produces.) Unable to cope with such a hostile environment, yeast succumbs to the terminal 'stationary' phase.

Reaching this point, when the yeast has converted virtually all the sugars into alcohol, usually takes 48 hours. Fermentation can then be ended by draining the wash (i.e. alcoholic liquid) from the fermentation vessels. The wash has an alcoholic strength of around 8% abv, and a cereal, biscuit, fruity character.

Fermentation can also be allowed to continue and begin a subsequent malolactic fermentation. Malolactic refers to lactic acid bacteria, which is naturally present in the wort (and sours milk, for example). This bacteria competes with the surviving yeast cells for any remaining sugars and nutrients. Yeast cells also begin to autolyse (rupture) and the contents, including nutrients, alcohol and flavour compounds, are released into the wash, which the lactic acid bacteria can devour (and in this strange twist of fate, yeast nourishes its nemesis). Lactic acid has no effect on phenolic compounds, but does create a range of additional flavour compounds, particularly fruit notes.

Fermentation takes place in a washback (a large vessel with a lid), which is either stainless steel or wooden. A significant difference between the two is that wooden washbacks (typically Oregon pine) host a higher bacterial population than stainless steel, principally lactic acid bacteria, and this additional influence is one reason for using wooden washbacks.

The importance of fermentation is creating a range of flavours that can be retained, or excluded, from the new make spirit during distillation. Up to 80 per cent of the flavours in new make spirit are attributed to fermentation; the longer the fermentation time, which can exceed 100 hours, the greater the range of flavour compounds created.

Distillation

In theory, distillation is a simple process: separating alcohol from water. When the wash is heated and reaches 78°C (172°F), alcohol begins to vaporize, whereas water vaporizes at 100°C (212°F). Alcohol vapours rise up the neck of the still and exit through the lyne arm. This copper pipe leads the vapours to a condenser, where a colder temperature causes the vapours to condense back into liquid, which drains from the base of the condenser.

However, each stage entails complex reactions that influence the spirit character. The first of two distillations takes place in a wash still, essentially a pragmatic process to increase the alcoholic strength from around 8% to 20–25% abv. This also helps to establish the overall flavour profile, including fruit, cereal and biscuit notes, together with phenolic compounds (if peated). The result of the first distillation is known as the low wines. The residue, an oily water known as spent lees, settles in the pot (the base of the still). Spent lees also contain a certain amount of phenolics, which means a lower level going forward to the second distillation.

Conducted in a spirit still, this is a far more creative process, as the distiller selects the flavour profile of the new make spirit. During the distillation run, the alcoholic strength of the distillate initially rises, peaking at around 80% abv, then gradually decreases. As the alcoholic strength changes, so does the character of the resulting spirit, from undesirable to desirable and then back to undesirable again. Each of these three phases has its own terminology, beginning with the heads (or foreshots), followed by the spirit cut and culminating in the tails. The heads and tails contain undesirable characteristics and are directed to a separate vessel, the low wines and feints receiver. The spirit cut, which contains desirable characteristics, is collected in the spirit receiver, and this is the new make spirit that is filled into casks for ageing.

Directing and redirecting the distillate from one receiver to another happens within the spirit safe. This resembles a glass 'display case' with an elegant brass frame for maximum visibility, containing a movable spout above two neighbouring basins. Distillate flows from the spout, and moving a lever is all it takes to reposition the spout and redirect the flow of distillate from one basin to another. From each basin the distillate drains into a different vessel, either the spirit receiver or the low wines and feints receiver.

The heads are the initial oily, pungent spirit, which contains toxic components such as methanol and has a cloudy appearance. The heads can last for 10–15 minutes or longer until the spirit runs clear.

The spirit cut can begin once desirable characteristics appear. Initially, this means elegant, floral and fruit notes, together with mellow smoky, medicinal phenolics. The spirit becomes progressively richer and fuller-bodied including cereal notes, although there isn't a convenient progression of light-medium-rich phenolics. Guaiacol tends to come over before phenols and cresols, with the sequence of smoky, medicinal notes leading to drier, earthier, more complex smoky bacon notes.

When to cut (change) from heads to the spirit cut and then to tails depends on each distillery's house style. A spirit cut beginning, for example, at 75% abv and ending at 65% abv results in new make spirit at 70% abv, with a more elegant, fruity character and lighter phenolics.

The lower the alcoholic strength of the new make spirit, the richer it is, including fuller-bodied phenolics.

Deciding exactly when to make the cut to tails when distilling peated spirit is complicated by the fact that the volume and complexity of phenolics escalate later in the distillation run, and soon overlap with undesirable oily, pungent characteristics. Consequently, it's a case of the best compromise, and which desirable and undesirable characteristics are lost and gained.

Tails have an additional significance. Prior to the second distillation, the low wines are combined with the heads and tails from the previous distillation. As heads contain lighter phenolics, while tails include richer phenolics, this increases the concentration of phenolic compounds. Consequently, a higher proportion end up in the new make spirit, enhancing the phenolic character.

Apart from the spirit cut, the profile of the new make spirit also depends on various other factors, such as the length of the neck rising from the pot (base) of the still. Lighter flavour compounds vaporize at lower temperatures than richer flavour compounds, which are physically heavier and require a higher temperature to vaporize. When vapours ascend a longer neck, they experience progressively lower temperatures, which are not hot enough to keep richer flavour compounds in a vapour form, causing them to condense and trickle back down the neck of the still into the pot. Meanwhile, lighter flavour compounds remain in vapour form despite the decreasing temperature and continue to the condenser. This process is known as reflux, and the greater the degree of reflux, the higher the proportion of lighter flavour compounds in the resulting spirit. Correspondingly, vapours ascending a shorter neck experience a smaller decrease in temperature, enabling a higher proportion of richer flavour compounds to continue to the condenser.

Another factor is the interaction between vapours and the copper surface of the still. For example, sulphur compounds (produced during fermentation) span vegetal, sweaty, meaty, struck-match notes that 'smother' lighter fruitiness and sweetness. However, copper has a 'matrix' on the surface that traps and retains sulphur compounds. Lowering the level of sulphur compounds in this way has a major influence, as lighter notes are 'unmasked' and become visible in the resulting new make spirit. Acids present in the vapours also interact with copper, creating additional esters (fruity notes).

Lyne arms

The lyne arm (or lye pipe), which connects the still to the condenser, is also made of copper, and so hosts the same interactions with vapours. The longer the lyne arm, the greater the degree of contact between the vapours and the copper, but also the greater the temperature differential between each end, and the greater the degree of reflux. If the lyne arm is angled upwards, it is less likely that any vapours condensing into liquid will reach the condensers. If the angle is downward, it is more likely that liquid will reach the condenser. The lyne arm can also be horizontal, which means a bit of both.

Condensers

The usual choice of condenser is a 'shell and tube', introduced in the 1880s. The original type, a worm, is still used by some distilleries in Scotland, but only by Ardnahoe on Islay.

A shell and tube condenser comprises a stainless steel cylinder, positioned vertically like a column, which contains numerous copper pipes running the length of the condenser. Water at the ambient temperature enters the base of the condenser, then rises up through the pipes and exits from the top. When hot vapours enter the condenser and come into contact with the cold pipes, they begin condensing and liquid trickles down the pipes, draining from the base of the condenser. Meanwhile, heat from the vapours transfers through the pipes to the water, which exits the condenser at a higher temperature.

A worm is a long, coiled copper pipe that forms decreasing circles and which reduces in diameter, housed within a large vessel called a worm tub. Cold water enters the base of the worm tub to cool the worm, and in turn cool the vapours, which condense into liquid and continue to the end of the worm from where they drain. Water rises and exits from the top of the worm tub, having been warmed by the heat of the worm.

Being a single copper pipe, a worm provides a smaller surface area of copper for the vapours to interact with, compared to the numerous pipes in a shell and tube condenser. This means that new make spirit using a worm has a relatively higher level of sulphur compounds, resulting in a richer, bolder house style.

The ageing process

How the new make spirit matures depends on the combined influence of various factors, including the choice of cask and alcoholic strength of the spirit when filled into the cask, the length of ageing and conditions within the ageing warehouse.

Filling at distillation strength (usually around 70% abv) was standard practice until the 1960s but is now rare, with 63.5% abv customary. This means adding water to reduce the strength. The filling strength also influences the range of flavour compounds that the spirit extracts from the cask. At 63.5% abv, the new make spirit contains 63.5 per cent alcohol and almost 36.5 per cent water. Flavour compounds within the oak staves of the cask, such as vanillin (which gives vanilla notes) are more water-soluble, while tannins (which enhance mouthfeel and add dryness) are more alcohol-soluble. A higher alcoholic strength means a greater propensity to extract alcohol-soluble compounds. Correspondingly, a lower strength contains higher proportions of water and extracts more water-soluble flavour compounds.

The alcoholic strength decreases during the ageing process, which means the proportion of alcohol and water is continually changing, albeit gradually. However, many flavour compounds are amenable to both alcohol and water, so making any definitive statements is challenging.

The range of flavour compounds a cask has to offer depends on the type of oak and its history before reaching the distillery. The archetypal choices are bourbon barrels (which occupy the most space in ageing warehouses) and sherry casks.

Cask selection

Bourbon barrels are made from 75–100 year old American oak trees felled in the forests of the Ozark and Arkansas regions, and sawn into lengths in order to dry the sap (which would otherwise compromise the resulting barrel). Air-drying, in the open, takes around 12 months, during which tannins leach from the wood, while microbacterial activity develops fruit and spice notes.

The timber is then cut into staves and made into barrels at a cooperage, where the interior is charred by applying a naked flame. Charring levels are on a scale of 1–4. A number 1 char means around 5 seconds of flaming, creating a char about 2 mm thick, which resembles burned toast. A number 2 and 3 char take progressively longer, with a number 4 char requiring around a minute, resulting in a layer of char up to 4 mm thick.

The heat of charring also toasts a couple of millimetres of the underlying oak, which activates flavour compounds, particularly vanillin. This contributes vanilla and variations such as crème caramel and crème brûlée to the maturing spirit. The initial beneficiary of these flavours is bourbon, which is aged for a minimum of two years, and as bourbon regulations stipulate that a barrel can only be used once, there is a constant supply to sell. The appeal of these barrels for malt whisky producers is that they have been 'seasoned' by ageing bourbon, which prevents the oak from dominating, while retaining a plentiful amount of flavour compounds.

Sherry casks are usually shipped to Scotland having been 'seasoned to order', with each detail stipulated in a contract with a bodega (sherry producer). The choice of oak includes American, which has a mellower influence and abundant vanilla, or Spanish oak, characterized by more intense dried fruit, spice and tannins. Sherry casks are toasted on the inside using a gentler process than charring, with the temperature and length of toasting developing different levels of vanilla, caramel and nougat flavours. The casks are seasoned for about two years, typically with Oloroso sherry, which gives more fruit and less spice than other styles of sherry, although the richness and intense raisin notes of Pedro Ximénez are increasingly utilized.

The impact of flavours a cask contributes depends on various factors. An elegant, unpeated or lightly peated malt can acquire up to 60–70 per cent of its character from the cask. The equivalent figure for a medium or heavily peated malt is lower, at around 40 per cent, as the intensity of phenolics 'overlays' flavours derived from the cask.

The size of the cask is another factor. Sherry casks are either hogsheads (250-litre (55-gallon) capacity) or butts (500 litres (110 gallons)), whereas bourbon barrels are 200 litres (44 gallons). The smaller the cask, the less liquid it contains, but the surface area contact between the liquid and the oak is proportionately greater, which increases the influence of the cask. This means casks can be selected according to their degree of influence. A traditional smaller size is a quarter cask (125 litres (27 gallons)), which has an intense impact, and is one of the cask types used for Laphroaig Quarter Cask.

The influence of a cask also depends on the 'fill', which refers to the number of times it has been used to age whisky. When filled for the first time, it is a first fill, for a second time it's a second fill, with three to four fills usually the limit. The number of fills a cask can provide varies, as does the length of each fill – it could be 10 or 20 years. This depends on the potential of each individual cask, which is assessed during maturation and after it is emptied.

Each fill extracts a particular level of flavour compounds from the oak, changing the level and balance of flavours gained by subsequent fills. A first-fill bourbon barrel gives distinct vanilla with a background of honeyed sweetness, whereas a second fill provides more evenly balanced vanilla, coconut and sweetness. Similarly, a first-fill Pedro Ximénez sherry cask contributes rich, syrupy sweetness, while a second fill gives more spice, particularly cinnamon, clove and aniseed.

First-fill casks also have the greatest impact on the 'distillery character' (i.e. the new make spirit), whereas a second fill allows a more even balance between the cask influence and the distillery character. This means that each fill is different but equally valid, and a recipe of different fills provides more scope for a master blender.

A broad range of casks, beyond bourbon and sherry, creates further flavour opportunities: for example, port and Madeira casks (either 225 litres/49 gallons or 500 litres/110 gallons), as well as Bordeaux and Sauternes wine barriques (225 litres/49 gallons). Each cask type makes its own particular contribution – Sauternes, for example, adds luscious apple, honey and tarte tatin notes.

As soon as a cask is filled with new make spirit, a complex series of reactions and interactions begins, including evaporation of water and alcohol from the cask, and oxidation (when air enters the cask and interacts with the spirit). The process is so intricate that it's not fully understood, though it has been established that phenolics don't interact with other compounds, or experience any modification. This is very unusual, and tannins are possibly the only other compound to make the same claim.

As the ageing process continues, the level of phenolics remains consistent, but appears to decrease. This is due to the growing level of other flavours, which the spirit is continually acquiring from the cask, including fruit and oak notes. But the flavour that most successfully diminishes the perception of phenolics is vanilla, which bourbon barrels provide in far greater quantities than sherry casks.

Islay malts also display a maritime character, with aromas of sea breeze, sea spray and brine, and sea salt and brine on the palate. The source of these characteristics has long been debated. 'It's from the peat,' say some. 'It's sea air entering the cask,' say others. And, of course, it could be both. Most Islay distilleries are positioned on the coastline, with a number of ageing warehouses having seafront locations, and some warehouse walls even experience direct contact with the sea, as at both Bowmore and Laphroaig.

A sea breeze is created when waves break and form foam, which consists of tiny bubbles containing aerosols (microdroplets) of seawater. When the bubbles burst, the aerosols are liberated, swept up and carried away by the breeze. Aerosols feature a rich recipe of sodium chloride, iodine, sulphate, calcium, potassium and iodine. But the most conspicuous ingredient is dimethyl sulphide, a gas produced by algae, which provides the distinctive aroma.

The extent to which sea breeze enters ageing warehouses depends on the opportunities provided: the number of vents, for example, which varies even among warehouses on the same site; the amount of windows and how often they are open, and how long the door remains open. Bowmore's no. 1 vault, for example, has no ventilation or windows, with the entrance door the only way in.

Sea air can enter ageing warehouses, but can salt from sea air pass through a barrel stave and season the maturing spirit within? The distance that has to be navigated is 25 mm (1in) in a bourbon barrel and 28–30 mm (1¼in) in a sherry cask. This may not seem much of a journey, but there's no direct route through a stave. It's a case of passing through various channels, including numerous pores (effectively voids that liquid can fill). But these are not arranged in a straight line; they're more like a maze, leading from side to side as well as forward. Another complication is that a stave has three zones: external, central and internal. Liquid and vapour can pass through the external and internal zones, but it is thought that only vapour can pass through the central zone.

Water from the atmosphere that condenses onto a cask, for example, can enter the external zone in liquid form, then pass through the central zone as vapour, and continue in liquid form to reach the maturing spirit within the cask. Water and alcohol within the spirit do the same in reverse, emerging on the surface of the cask as tiny bubbles, then evaporating into the atmosphere.

Salt is not volatile, so cannot pass through the central zone in vapour form. However, if this zone is saturated with liquid, which dripping walls in a humid warehouse could facilitate, this would enable a salt solution to pass through and reach the spirit within the cask. The central zone is much narrower than the external and internal zones, which increases the possibility of saturation. A salt solution could also potentially seep through gaps between joints and staves, which would be a short-cut to the spirit. But the number of gaps is limited, and whether enough could seep through to make a discernible difference is uncertain. These possibilities continue to be debated and studied, as current research has not been able to prove or disprove the theory that sea air influences the spirit.

Another aspect of this debate is that casks contain potassium and calcium, both of which are capable of suggesting sea salt. Consequently, sodium needn't be present for a malt whisky to seem seasoned with salt. However, casks also contain sodium, which complicates this!

Evaporation and oxidation are two other significant influences, with evaporation having an impact from year one, while oxidation takes several years to make a discernible difference. Evaporation of water and alcohol from the cask averages around 1.5–2 per cent per annum on Islay, which continually reduces the volume of spirit. Although evaporation has such a measurable impact in terms of losses, its influence on the ageing process is still being researched. This means that current definitions of evaporation don't go beyond generalizations, such as concentrating, mellowing and refining the flavour profile.

As the volume of spirit decreases, a headspace develops between the surface of the liquid and the top of the cask, and evaporation sees the headspace continually increasing. Air accumulates within this headspace, having passed through pores in the oak and tiny gaps between the staves and joints of the cask. Air also enters the cask below the surface of the liquid, and is 'absorbed' by the spirit, instigating oxidation. One effect of oxidation is creating acids in the spirit, which subsequently react with alcohol to create esters (fruit notes). Other consequences of oxidation remain uncertain beyond a 'refining effect' that enhances complexity.

Climate

'If you don't like the weather, just wait five minutes' is an Islay phrase I've frequently heard. Depending on where you are, and how extensive the vista, you can see the weather in the distance. I've stood in rain but seen blue sky and sunshine ahead, hoping it would soon reach me.

The weather plays a significant role in Islay life, and also in the life of malt whisky (sheltering in an ageing warehouse doesn't make the climate irrelevant). There are two types of ageing warehouse, readily identifiable from a distance. Dunnage warehouses are traditional, low-rise buildings with stone walls and slate roofs, the equivalent of 'country manor' accommodation. Racked warehouses are high-rise and typically metal clad, resembling urban apartment blocks.

The temperature from December to March varies on average from 2 to 9°C (36°F to 48°F). In April it's 4–11°C (39–52°F), while from May to September the temperature rarely peaks beyond 17°C (63°F), and in October ranges from 7 to 13°C (45°F to 55°F). Rainfall averages 200 days per year, and exceeds 130 cm (4 ft) in total, with January to February the wettest and March to September the driest. Humidity rises in June, peaks in July and August, then decreases in October. From November to February winds can average 20mph, and 12mph in June and July.

That's the external weather. What matters is how this influences the climate inside ageing warehouses. Warmer air holds more moisture than colder air, and when warm, humid air enters a warehouse it cools and condenses, landing on the floor, walls and casks (where it can be absorbed). Additionally, a well-ventilated warehouse clears moisture from the atmosphere more rapidly than a less-ventilated warehouse. Warmer temperatures mean faster evaporation rates and, in fact, an acceleration in the rate of all reactions.

Dunnage warehouses have thick stone walls that minimize temperature changes, while earthen floors enhance humidity. Windows and vents provide air flow, which helps promote more consistent temperatures throughout the warehouse. Casks are typically stacked three high, meaning each level experiences (essentially) the same conditions. Overall, conditions in dunnage warehouses promote more gradual maturation.

Racked warehouses transmit climatic conditions to the casks far more than dunnage. As casks can be stacked eight to ten high on special racks, casks at the top experience warmer temperatures in summer and colder temperatures in winter, and lower humidity compared to casks on the ground floor. This means the rate of development varies; casks on the lower floors lose more alcohol than water through evaporation, which lowers the alcoholic strength, and can promote elegance and sweetness. On the upper floors, more water than alcohol evaporates, leading to a richer, rounder style.

Chapter Three

Deconstructing malt whisky

Chapter Three

Deconstructing malt whisky

It's incredible that a sip of malt whisky can contain so many characteristics. Around 100 flavour compounds have been identified in malt whisky, though it's a moving total as research is ongoing, and the technology to analyse malt whisky continues to evolve. The impact of flavour compounds is all the more remarkable considering that a malt whisky bottled at 40% abv (alcohol by volume) comprises 40 per cent alcohol – with the balance essentially water – while flavour compounds account for less than 1 per cent of the total.

The levels of flavour compounds such as esters (fruit), vanillin, which provides vanilla flavours, and phenolics are measured in parts per million, abbreviated to ppm: 1 ppm is equivalent to 1 milligram in a litre. Peating levels are routinely quoted by distilleries, and typically peak at 40–50 ppm (see page 34). Levels of other flavour compounds are not quoted.

Malty, digestive biscuit notes, derived from barley, are measured in parts per billion: 1 ppb is equivalent to 1 microgram per litre. Even compounds measured in parts per trillion (ppt), such as cork taint and sulphur compounds (manifested as rubber, struck match, vegetal notes, sweaty trainers), are discernible. The level is not the decisive factor; it's how active a compound is that matters.

Flavour compounds can also be present at such low levels that they are not individually discernible, but nevertheless make a contribution.

Phenolic compounds below 2 ppm are usually 'invisible' in terms of smoke and peat, but can add sweetness, which provides a further benefit by enhancing the perception of fruit flavours.

This is why analysing a malt whisky to identify and measure the level of flavour compounds doesn't indicate the resulting flavour profile, as this depends on how the flavours interact. Similarly, listing flavour compounds within Islay malts would show a significant overlap between distilleries. But the varying levels of these compounds and how they interact ensure a unique result for each malt whisky.

Flavour compounds also contribute significantly to mouthfeel, essentially due to their size, the molecules being larger than water and alcohol molecules. The level and combination of different flavour compounds determine the mouthfeel, which explains why this varies so much among malts.

Vanillin, for example, creates a soft, silky, creamy texture, while fatty acid esters give a smooth, fuller-bodied mouthfeel. The level of fatty acid esters varies from one malt to another. They originate during fermentation, particularly when using wooden rather than stainless steel washbacks, and in greater quantities when fermentation times are longer. Fatty acid esters also appear slightly later in the distillation run because they are larger, weightier molecules, so the spirit cut also determines the level of fatty acid esters.

However, it's tannins that have always been hailed for enhancing mouthfeel, though whether this is entirely justified remains uncertain. European oak contains significantly higher tannin levels than American oak, with a first fill containing higher levels than a second fill. And as the level of tannins and other flavour compounds and the interaction between them continually evolve during the ageing process, the mouthfeel is also subject to change.

The role of alcohol

Alcohol plays a diverse role, ranging from the physiological effects of drinking alcohol, which are readily discernible, to the influence on the character of a malt whisky, which is more elusive.

Alcohol adds body and weight, enhancing the sense of mouthfeel, and although alcohol doesn't contribute flavour, beyond a hint of sweetness, it determines the flavours a malt whisky shows. This is because flavour compounds are either soluble or insoluble at varying alcoholic strengths. When a flavour compound is soluble, it's 'dissolved' in the alcohol, and the flavour isn't discernible. When a flavour compound is insoluble, it exists independently of the whisky, and is discernible. There isn't, however, an on/off switch at particular strengths for different compounds. Flavours gradually emerge, reach a peak of visibility, then slowly fade over a range of alcoholic strengths. Some compounds, phenolics for example, change more at varying alcoholic strengths than others, such as esters.

Consequently, the bottling strength plays a vital role. The minimum is 40% abv, with 43% abv traditional in export markets. More recently, 46% abv has become established, as this is the lowest bottling strength possible without having to chill-filter. Below this strength a cloudy haze can form if the malt reaches a colder temperature. The haze is caused by fatty acid esters coming out of solution and so becoming physically visible, which can be removed by chilling the malt and passing it through a filter. As fatty acid esters also contribute to mouthfeel and character, whether and to what extent chill-filtering creates any change is a major talking point. And the fact that there are various degrees of chill-filtering, including very gentle, have added further nuance to the debate.

Cask-strength malts, bottled at the strength they reach in the cask, are prized for being the most 'natural' expression (on the basis that no water is added) and span a range of alcoholic strengths. An amazing example is Caol Ila unpeated 15 year old, one of the Special Releases of 2016, bottled at 61.5% abv.

Cask-strength bottlings have a growing following, but the majority of malts are bottled at a predetermined strength, which is reached by diluting with water.

The role of water

When I started exploring malt whisky in the late 1980s, a distillery's water source was hailed as a significant factor in the individuality of a malt whisky. Images of pristine streams and serene lochs were an engaging, accessible concept. The reality is that water plays a major role in the production process, to facilitate mashing, providing steam to heat the stills and to cool the condensers, but water plays a far less significant role in the resulting flavour.

As an ingredient in malt whisky, water is used to dilute new make spirit when filling casks. Similarly, water is used to adjust the alcoholic strength of mature whisky for bottling. This water is typically demineralized – meaning the level of minerals is lowered through filtration. As minerals give water its character and texture, whether and to what extent demineralized water can contribute to the character of a malt whisky is uncertain. But it can't be ruled out. Another aspect of this debate is that knowing a malt whisky contains water from a specific source, particularly if exclusive to a distillery, can have an emotional impact.

What happens when we taste malt whisky?

There are various ways to enjoy malt whisky: you can simply sit back, sip and savour the flavours and feelings this creates. Tasting can also, of course, be a more disciplined experience, in which the aroma, mouthfeel, flavours and the finish (aftertaste) are analysed. Either approach involves a complex process during which the senses send messages to the brain – the only difference is whether this is undertaken consciously or unconsciously.

Even before inhaling or sampling a malt whisky, the brain is already evaluating visual information. The bottle and label are, of course, designed to appeal and engage; which means the more I like it, the greater my expectations. And if the whisky doesn't match those expectations, I'm disappointed. But this is ridiculous! I shouldn't be judging a malt whisky against my expectations, only on the flavour profile. This is why I try to prevent my brain from conducting any detective work before I begin tasting.

Exactly how different parts of the brain process information, individually and collectively and reach conclusions is only partially understood. Messages are transmitted from the nose (technically the olfactory sense), the palate and the retronasal passage (located at the back of the throat, linking the palate to the nose/olfactory sense), and the throat to the brain, which then collates all the information and tries to reach a conclusion.

The olfactory sense

Olfactory receptors at the summit of each nasal cavity receive all the credit for detecting aroma, which makes it easy to underestimate the nostrils. However, nostrils play a fascinating role as a conduit, with one nostril always experiencing greater air flow than the other, which intensifies the experience for the olfactory receptors in that nostril. Which nostril is the superhighway changes every 30 minutes. (If only there was an app that could indicate which it is and when, it would really benefit the process of tasting.)

Olfactory receptors comprise about 400 separate groups, most of which react to more than one aroma, though one aroma can stimulate numerous groups simultaneously. Messages from olfactory receptors in each nostril are posted separately to different parts of the brain. Receptors in the left nostril reach the left hemisphere, while the right nostril transmits to the right hemisphere of the brain. From these separate hemispheres, messages are sent to the olfactory bulb, which conducts some identification work, but also enhances the quality of the messages, and forwards them to other parts of the brain for further analysis. The objective is to identify the aroma and provide a context for it by drawing on the memory bank.

The palate

Whatever appears in the aroma is utilized by the brain as advance information about the palate. This creates expectations, which can result in the palate being judged against these expectations rather than its own merits. The aroma can give an indication of flavour, but extrovert aromas can also lead to a quiet palate, or vice versa. To be as objective as possible, I focus on the aroma as a separate event from the palate, and only consider the relationship between them once I've finished tasting.

The palate has three components: the tongue, the soft palate (including gums, cheeks and back of the roof of the mouth) and the retronasal passage.

The tongue is the most accomplished of this trio, and first into action gauging mouthfeel, which is determined exclusively by the tongue using its nervous system.

Flavour compounds are also assessed by the tongue, using papillae (tiny protrusions) that have a porous surface, allowing liquid and flavour compounds to pass through and reach taste receptors within the taste buds. A single taste bud contains up to 150 different taste receptors, with each receptor identifying one or more characteristics, including sweetness, sourness, salt, umami and bitterness. Each taste bud can also have a number of receptors that detect the same flavour.

An average tongue is equipped with 2,000–5,000; the total varies by 20–25 per cent among the population. Whether 'supertasters' (who are unusually sensitive to flavours) have greater quantities of taste papillae is uncertain. And the extent to which this could provide an advantage is also unclear. What's definitely a vital factor is the brain's ability to interpret information received from taste receptors.

The gums and cheeks of the soft palate (so called as bones are absent) play a supporting role, as they lack taste receptors. However, the soft palate utilizes the underlying nervous system to identify characteristics such as smoothness, dryness, pepperiness and astringency, rather than flavours. Consequently, the soft palate can supplement information sent from taste receptors in the tongue.

When assessing malt whisky on the palate, the liquid is warmed and reaches body temperature (37°C/98.6°F). This leads to phenolic compounds, vanillin and esters (fruit notes) evaporating from the liquid and making their way to the throat, then ascending the retronasal passage. There isn't any assessment work undertaken in this passage; it's simply a route for vapours to reach the olfactory receptors. The same aromas that reach the olfactory receptors from malt whisky in a glass also reach them from the palate. We may think the most important location is the palate, but the olfactory sense is actually doing the majority of the work. However, the palate has a significant influence on phenolics.

'Saliva coats some phenolics and prevents them from evaporating and revealing their character. What level of phenolics may be lost due to this is uncertain,' says Professor Barry Smith, director of the Institute of Philosophy and Centre for the Study of the Senses.

The phenolics lost at this stage are subsequently regained, but in a different region. 'Swallowing warms the phenolics further, making them more volatile, and able to rise up from the throat and travel further into the nose, with guaiacol tending to come through more than other phenolic compounds. This is perceived as an aftertaste, but is actually more of an after-smell,' continues Professor Smith.

The throat actually hosts further, complementary reactions. 'Bacteria in the throat, which are there to protect against infections, interact with flavour compounds to produce new compounds, which also means that additional nuances can show in phenolics as a result of other flavours being muted or boosted by this interaction,' he remarks.

Phenolic compounds also contribute to the perception of dryness, together with tannins, though neither actually adds dryness. As Professor Smith explains, 'Tannins pucker the mouth and give a dry feeling. What actually happens is that the tannins coagulate the proteins in saliva which creates friction, and this is perceived as dryness, but dryness is a texture we feel, not a taste.'

One of the great joys of assessing a malt whisky is 'visualizing' it as much as analysing the characteristics. I see the flavours in my mind as horizontal layers. Sweetness and citrus, for example, are the top layers, oak and dryness the base layers, with fruit and vanilla the central layer (the big picture resembles a Victoria sponge cake).

The second sip of a malt clarifies the picture. This is partly due to the palate having acclimatized to the alcohol, and flavours such as sweetness accruing. But it's also due to the brain adjusting. The first sip provides a lot of information for the brain to grapple with. The second sip gives the brain more detail, particularly subtler nuances, which supplements knowledge gained from the first sip.

The information sent to the brain about the same malt whisky inevitably varies from one person to another, as we are all more sensitive to some characteristics, and less sensitive to others. The greatest divergence of sensitivity and insensitivity applies to citrus, phenolic compounds, bitterness and cork taint. This means that what a malt whisky has to offer depends on the characteristics we are able to perceive from it. Each of us may pick up the same, or similar or different characteristics from the same malt whisky.

The feelings that malt whisky generates is another amazing part of the experience, and I'm researching the source of these emotions. Are they triggered by the brain, and specifically the memory? The brain identifies flavours on the basis of memory, in which case does memory provide a repeat of previous emotions that followed a sip of an enjoyable malt whisky? Do such feelings come from the (metaphorical) heart? Being a romantic, I think so.

Tasting techniques

My approach to tasting is based on what I've learned from numerous tastings given by master blenders, master distillers and distillery managers, to which I added my own extras. Techniques provide a structure, and then what's required is experience and practice. I regularly open jars of herbs and spices, and hold fruit under my nose to consolidate my memory bank. And whether it's malt whisky, a cup of coffee or lemon tart served with a scoop of vanilla ice cream, it's all a valid experience, as tasting is all about identifying aromas, flavours, mouthfeel and aftertaste, and finding the right words to describe them.

Gauging aroma

Gently rotating a glass to roll the whisky languidly around the bowl is enough to release the aromas. The traditional practice of swirling unleashes alcohol, which attacks the olfactory sense and then entails waiting for the alcohol to subside.

Nosing a few inches above the glass confirms whether the whisky is releasing aroma or spirit; if the latter, allow the sample to settle down before trying again. Once I pick up aroma, I go in a little deeper, inhale and see what I find. The aroma could be integrated, with a range of notes appearing simultaneously, or there can be a sequence of individual notes, some at the forefront and others at the edges.

My nose doesn't stay in the glass for long, as the nose becomes saturated with alcohol quite quickly, so going in and out of the glass gives the nose short breaks, and enables me to detect whether anything has changed since my previous visit.

Palate

I like to hold the whisky on my tongue for a few seconds, as a primary test to gauge how it feels, and texture is the first characteristic evident on the palate. Then I start to move the whisky around my palate, taking in a little air from the side of my mouth, and see what happens.

A malt may begin very quietly and gradually open up, or it can announce itself with an immediate fanfare. The characteristics can be integrated, with equally balanced notes appearing simultaneously. Or there can be a sequence of individual notes, some primary, others secondary, fleeting or longer-term. The degree of evolution is also fascinating to experience, with sweetness usually appearing at an early stage together with vanilla and fruit notes. Midway is often a turning point with dryness emerging.

How sweetness and dryness complement each other is another factor, with the contrast between them creating a greater sense of structure and range. I find sweetness is usually more intense, with dryness a subtler, underlying note. Sweetness makes other flavours such as vanilla seem more indulgent, and fruit appears riper, while dryness emphasizes other flavours through contrast.

Sweetness and dryness can also combine to create richness, which provides an additional indulgence.

The finish generally begins with dryness, which sometimes emerges gently and grows, or is immediately forthright, before other notes join in. These may be the same characteristics in the same order and with the same balance as the palate, or the balance and sequence can change; characteristics that are subtle on the palate may appear more intense in the finish, or vice versa. Ideally, more enjoyable flavour should come through, otherwise it's not going to encourage another sip.

Tasting notes

A tasting note can be instinctive and simply state a verdict: 'I love it.' But it's interesting to say why, for the benefit of others, or just for yourself!

The least informative tasting notes are lists of generalizations: elegant, mellow, balanced. These terms are fine, of course, but with context. Another style of tasting note that tells only part of the story is the shopping list of flavours: fruity, spicy, peaty, smoky, oaky. This is a concise overview, but doesn't differentiate between primary and secondary flavours, or describe the interaction between them.

A tasting note written in prose rather than note form gives a far greater sense of what is happening in real time. By deconstructing the flavour profile, differentiating primary and secondary flavours, describing how they evolve, stipulating when sweetness and dryness appear and the effect this has, tasting notes effectively write themselves, and will be evocative and accessible.

An interesting option is to add a 'conceptual' conclusion to a tasting note, evoking the personality of a malt whisky and how it makes you feel rather than stipulating flavours. A malt can appear elegantly attired and accessorized; commanding but yielding; muscular and animated.

The vocabulary of tasting notes has become far more detailed and extensive in the past 20 years, which highlights another element of tasting notes: clear communication. And as other aspects of tasting are increasingly discussed, such as the influence of glassware, the differences between the first and subsequent sips of a malt and the effect of dilution, tasting notes may become far more comprehensive. In time, it could become standard practice to include 'qualifiers', stipulating the style of glassware used, how much water was added (if applicable) to what volume of malt whisky and whether the tasting note is based on the first sip, the second sip or a medley. And then we will have even more to discuss with each other!

Glassware

Choosing an attractive glass from which to enjoy a malt whisky doesn't mean I'm shallow. Drinking a malt whisky is an event, and I would like a glass with the appropriate stature. A more profound reason for choosing a particular glass is that the size and shape influence the way aromas and flavours are channelled and perceived. It's a fascinating experiment to pour the same amount of malt whisky into different styles of glassware, then compare and contrast. Some flavours can be amplified or diminished, which means the same malt can taste subtly or significantly different, depending on the glass.

I prefer a small tulip-shaped tasting glass. But even this style of glassware includes bowls with different curves and dimensions. I compared the same Islay malt from two very similarly shaped tulip glasses, one slightly larger with a more curvaceous bowl. The smaller glass showed embers with a hint of coal, baked apples and vanilla on the nose, and a subtle brine note. The larger glass led with vanilla, underlying toast and more streamlined embers, and apple pie rather than baked apples. On the palate, the smaller glass delivered a more elegant experience; the larger glass delivered more weight and body. To use a musical analogy, played on a piano, malt from the smaller glass was a series of notes played higher up the keyboard.

Diluting

There's always the same question at a tasting: whether or not to add water. Diluters are encouraged to do this on the basis that water 'opens up' a malt whisky. This suggests that the malt remains the same but becomes more accessible with water. It's more accurate to say that adding water changes a malt, as alcoholic strength is a key influence in the flavours a malt whisky shows. The more water added, the greater the change. Exploring a favourite malt with varying degrees of dilution is a fascinating experiment, with a valuable result: finding the optimal amount of water for your palate.

If diluting, the water should be still spring water (which is neutral, so as not to affect the flavour of the spirit; the distinctive taste of mineral waters would add flavour). If adding water to older malts matured in sherry casks, it's vital to add water gradually in tiny amounts and see how it goes, as this style of malt is vulnerable and can collapse under the influence of water, which would be tragic after all those years of ageing.

Adding water to malt whisky prompts a major structural change. The main matrix is water and alcohol molecules, which form configurations or patterns. Alcohol molecules take the lead, forming their preferred configuration, then water molecules slot in where they can. Flavour compounds, including phenolics, then snuggle up in the remaining spaces. (I wish I had a handy viewing device to watch this happen.)

My preference is not to add water, as I love the intensity of higher-strength malts. The flavours have a certain magnificence, and the mouthfeel, a characteristic I greatly appreciate, can be super-soft. I do also taste malts with a drop of water for comparison. And although I've reached the same verdict for many years (undiluted is best!), I continue to approach this as objectively as possible.

One reason for preferring malts at bottling strength is that they generally reveal an individual sequence of flavours, which also evolves on the palate. I love tracking this change, as it's exciting to see what happens. Diluting malts generally makes them more integrated, with a tight package of flavours that cluster together. And the mouthfeel changes dramatically; I find it simply becomes watery, which is a tragic loss of individuality.

I compared a peated Islay malt at 40% abv, pouring the same quantity of malt into four glasses of the same size and shape. One glass remained undiluted, to another I added 1 teaspoon of water, 2 teaspoons of water to the next and 3 teaspoons to the fourth glass. Comparing the most immediate aromas from each glass, the neat sample showed rich embers and extra-virgin olive oil; with 1 teaspoon of water this became grassier, hay and woody; with 2 teaspoons of water there was a hint of toast, honey and citrus; with 3 teaspoons of water it was thick set honey, vanilla and toasted crumpets.

Comparing the palate, the neat sample showed chargrilled and barbecued notes, which opened up with fresh citrus and sea salt; with 1 teaspoon of water the chargrilled and toasted notes were integrated rather than separate, with hints of oak and dryness; with 2 teaspoons of water, the toasted notes were even more integrated, the dryness more evident and some citrus at the edges; with 3 teaspoons of water, the toasted notes were more like toasted bread with a hint of marmalade and light creaminess.

Storing and displaying whisky

Malt whisky only requires a few precautions to remain at its peak: bottles must be kept upright in cool, dry conditions and away from direct light. The extent to which malt whisky can change after a bottle is opened and whether any changes occur in an unopened bottle are current debates in the whisky world.

Monitoring changes in an opened bottle is straightforward; it just takes patience. A tasting note written as soon as a bottle is opened serves as a 'control', which can be compared to subsequent tasting notes (recording the date and the level of whisky in the bottle). Each time a sample is poured, the existing air in the headspace is expelled, and subsequently replaced by fresh air. And as the level of liquid decreases and the headspace increases, the opportunities for oxidation multiply and the more distinct the changes could be. An unopened bottle has a tiny headspace, so there is potential for change, but what is the experiment that can determine this?

Displaying malts raises questions and options, of a practical as well as an aesthetic nature. Besides keeping bottles standing upright away from direct light to remain in optimum condition, to give the greatest joy they need to be displayed like an exhibit. This raises the vital question of how they should be arranged. By country and by distillery is the most logical, with expressions in alphabetical order by name. But should bottlings that only have age statements be in a separate section from those that have names, or does 12 year old count as a 'T' and 15 year old count as an 'F' in the alphabetical order?

I'm not sure at the moment. My friends tell me that life's too short to spend time devising such a pedantic system. My reply is that life's too short to waste time searching for a particular bottling, when my system takes me straight there.

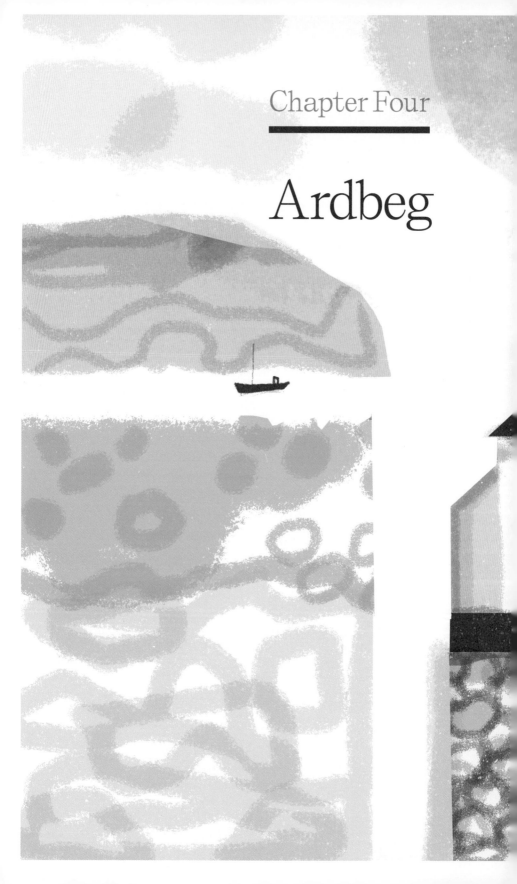

Chapter Four

Ardbeg

Chapter Four

Ardbeg

Distilleries are an integral part of the Islay landscape, which gives the malts a definite sense of place. One of Ardbeg's expressions, Corryvreckan, was named after a whirlpool that results from the sheer volume of seawater passing through the narrow constraints of the Sound of Islay (between Islay and Jura), which then continues along the Jura coastline and suddenly finds an opportunity to turn right through the straits of Corryvreckan, between Jura and the tiny island of Scarba. This may seem a convenient shortcut, but it's an obstacle course rather than an escape route. A sudden drop of 219 metres (240 yards) below the seabed, as though a trap door had opened, is followed by a basalt rock 130 metres (142 yards) high. The result is an extraordinary whirlpool.

How Islay, together with Jura and Scarba, was formed can be explained by geology, but for romantics mythology is preferable. It all began once upon a time when a Danish princess called Iula (pronounced *Yula*) longed to explore the world beyond her homeland. Born into a family of giants, she was able to stride majestically through the North Sea and head for Scotland. Following the coastline, Iula created a wonderful legacy. In her apron she carried a number of magic stones, which she periodically cast into the sea. Each stone expanded and gave rise to an island, with the final stone creating Islay. At this point a storm began to rage, and vast waves rose, overwhelming the princess. She was subsequently buried in a hillside on Islay by Loch Cnoc (when and by whom on such a recently created island is not recorded, but it's best not to question mythology). Loch Cnoc is not far from the Ardbeg distillery, which is affectionately termed 'the peaty paradox', reflecting the complexity of the malts created by supreme levels of peat, smoke and sweetness.

Origins and expressions

Ardbeg distillery was established in 1815 on the site of a former illicit distillery founded by the MacDougalls, a farming family living on Islay. As the distillery evolved, a village grew around it where workers and their families lived in cottages, with a cooperage, peat store and pier where puffers (coal-fired ships with one mast) could deliver supplies from the mainland and collect casks. The family employed distillery managers and emigrated to Canada at the end of the nineteenth century. The distillery remained in family ownership until 1959, when a different era began with a series of acquisitions, including one by Canadian drinks company Hiram Walker in 1977. Two years later, Allied Distillers merged with Hiram Walker. This brought Laphroaig into the same portfolio as Ardbeg, with Laphroaig the flagship malt that received more attention and investment.

In the early 1980s, a severe global recession saw demand for Scotch whisky slump, and inevitably resulted in a lack of investment. In 1981, the floor maltings were closed and the distillery was mothballed, with the loss of 17 jobs. However, from 1989 Ardbeg was back in production for three months a year, but not to cater for single malt demand: only 1–2 per cent of Ardbeg's annual production was bottled as a single malt. Ardbeg was an important ingredient in blended Scotch such as Ballantine's, and production continued on a limited basis during the 1990s, essentially to meet the demand for blends.

In June 1996, Ardbeg was put up for sale by Allied. Negotiations with the eventual buyer, Glenmorangie, led to a contract that contained a clause to continue supplying new make spirit to be aged for subsequent use in Ballantine's. The purchase was completed in February 1997, and included the remaining whisky stocks (distilled before 1981) in the ageing warehouses. Some of the original employees returned. Everything had to be repaired or renewed, and Glenmorangie invested £3 million in Ardbeg during the first year, when production reached 250,000 litres (55,000 gallons) under distillery manager Stuart Thomson.

A visitor centre followed in May 1998, together with a shop and restaurant, which was opened by Jackie Thomson, who had been working for Glenmorangie and relocated from the mainland to the town of Port Ellen in 1997. 'People thought it was mad to open a restaurant in a distillery, but it took off very quickly, and we soon had regulars, principally locals,' Jackie says. One local visitor who arrived on a daily basis from the nearby village of Ardbeg was Shortie, a Jack Russell terrier. 'Shortie used to sit by the door to the visitor centre, waiting for someone to open the door for him. He received a lot of attention from visitors, and was well fed,' adds Jackie. Shortie subsequently appeared in various promotions and was celebrated as a mascot for Ardbeg. But celebrity status didn't change him; he remained as friendly as ever. His portrait hangs in the restaurant showing him wearing a crown, a fitting tribute to a charming character.

By 1999, production had reached 600,000 litres (132,000 gallons) and momentum was growing in other ways too. Passionate Ardbeg fans began sending messages of support (the quickest method then was sending a fax). This led to the management forming the Ardbeg Committee in the year 2000, with a central promise that the doors of Ardbeg would never close again. Membership of the Committee was open to all Ardbeg fans, who registered their details and enjoyed the benefits. 'The Ardbeg Committee was a great way to start connecting with people, giving information through our newsletter Momentous Minutes, and absorbing information from members. There were special bottlings exclusive to Committee members, as well as invitations to special events. Membership grew rapidly worldwide,' says Jackie, who is the Ardbeg Committee chair.

Two notable rarities were Lord of the Isles, launched in 2001: a magnificent blend of casks distilled in 1976 and 1977, making this (unofficially) a 25 year old, and very much a senior Islay malt at that time; while Kildalton launched in 2004 was an unpeated example of Ardbeg. This was made possible because unpeated and lightly peated malted barley had been distilled in 1980 on an experimental basis, and the resulting malt featured fruit flavours at the forefront. Only 1,300 bottles were available, which could only be purchased at the distillery.

In 2007, Mickey Heads took over as distillery manager. His father was a still man at Port Ellen distillery, where his grandfather was head malt man. Mickey began his career in 1979, joining Laphroaig as a peat cutter, and was then head brewer from 1990 to 1999. That year he moved to the neighbouring Isle of Jura, where he was the distillery manager until 2007. In July of that year, having relocated to Ardbeg, Mickey celebrated the launch of Mor (Gaelic for 'big, mighty, magnificent'). It certainly was, being the largest bottle of single malt whisky released in Scotland: 52 cm (20in) high, weighing 6.5 kg (14lb) and containing 4.5 litres (1 gallon) of Ardbeg 10 year old, and this was the first time it was available at the cask strength of 57.3% abv.

Mor was all about being big, and Mickey soon had another big challenge to deal with. In November, the boiler broke down. It had been installed in 1968, so this lapse was hardly surprising. The team tried everything, but the boiler refused to cooperate. Meanwhile, eight washbacks full of fermented liquid were ready to be distilled. Without a working boiler the stills couldn't be heated, so it wasn't possible to distil. What to do? Mickey then rang Dr Bill Lumsden (Ardbeg's director of distilling and whisky creation) with even worse news. The parts needed for the boiler would arrive in three weeks. Bill decided to embrace destiny and told Mickey to remove the lids of the washbacks and open all the windows in the area, to provide access for natural airborne yeast and Islay air to participate in the process.

'I've always wanted to experiment with longer fermentations, so I think an unintentional boiler breakdown was the best thing that could have happened! For context, most Ardbeg is only fermented for 72 hours, making three weeks unchartered territory for us,' says Dr Lumsden.

The boiler recovered, the wash was distilled and produced a sharp, vibrant spirit, which was filled into casks. Then it was a case of waiting to see how it would mature. Patiently. For years. (See page 82.)

The distillery celebrated an important milestone in 2015: Ardbeg's 200th anniversary, marked by a special bottling, Perpetuum. This was distilled in 1971–2, when the peating levels were unusually low, and reflected the influence of bourbon barrels and sherry casks, which yielded dark chocolate and treacle with sea spray and peat smoke.

Mickey retired in 2020, and to commemorate his tenure Ardbeg released Arrrrrrrdbeg!, the distillery's first whisky wholly matured in ex-rye whisky casks. This provided a spicy mouthfeel with fruity flavours, while the long finish featured gentle lingering smoke. The bottle label, which depicted Mickey as a salty seadog, was created by Butcher Billy, a renowned Brazilian artist and graphic designer.

Colin Gordon was Mickey's successor. He had joined Caol Ila in 2013, and was at Port Ellen Maltings between 2015 and 2018, then at Lagavulin from 2018 to 2020, arriving at Ardbeg in 2020. Colin has probably worked at more Islay distilleries than anyone else, giving him a broad perspective and wealth of experience: 'I would say the most interesting thing about working in different distilleries on Islay is the history and the character of each, which makes them unique. I love the fact that all sites use peated malt (varying levels), water and yeast, but the depth and difference in each spirit is incredible. Ardbeg has a beautiful balance of smoke, herbal notes and citrus, Lagavulin has liquorice and earthiness, while Caol Ila is lighter and floral. This is the magic of Islay whisky.'

A new stillhouse became operational on 19 March 2021, with the first new make spirit running at 3.00 a.m. A traditional way of launching a new still is to 'sweeten it' with a handful of ingredients used in the production process. Colin placed a spade of peat into the still for a symbolic moment, before withdrawing it. This peat had been cut at Kintour Moss on the Ardtalla Estate, Ardbeg's traditional source of peat. The new stillhouse enabled production to almost double, from 1.4 million litres (308,000 gallons) per year to 2.4 million litres (527,900 gallons).

A tribute to the previous stillhouse, which remains intact, was released in 2021. This was referred to as Ardbeg's 'newest oldest whisky', since at 25 years old it is the oldest permanently available expression, albeit in limited quantities. When the spirit for this bottling was distilled in the 1990s, Ardbeg was only producing tiny quantities, which makes it extremely rare. 'After a quarter of a century in the cask, you'd be forgiven for imagining that Ardbeg 25 year old would have lost some of the hallmark Ardbeg smoky punch. I can assure you it hasn't. And yet there's also a remarkable complexity and elegance to this whisky that I find utterly captivating. It's unmistakably Ardbeg, but unlike any Ardbeg you've tasted before,' says Dr Lumsden.

Now, whatever happened to the spirit distilled from the excessively long fermentation, when the boiler broke down in 2007? The resulting distillate was aged for 13 years in first-fill and refill bourbon barrels, and released in 2022 as Ardbeg Fermutation. 'Peat and smoke meld with fresh, floral flavours, while sharper, malty notes give Ardbeg Fermutation an animated uniquely zingy profile,' Dr Lumsden reports.

Billed as the smokiest Ardbeg ever, Hypernova was released in October 2022, taking Ardbeg's signature smoke into a new dimension with peating levels in excess of 170 ppm and bottled at 51% abv. Creosote, soot and tar are among the aromas. The palate has chocolate sweetness, peppermint, peat smoke and a burst of aniseed and clove. The finish shows enormously heavy smoke, before returning to earthy notes of roasted coffee.

Another extraordinary highlight in 2022 was a cask of Ardbeg distilled in 1975 being sold to a private collector in Asia for £16 million, the highest auction price paid for a cask of single malt. Known as Cask No.

3, this is the oldest cask ever released by Ardbeg, and extremely rare, as so little single malt was distilled throughout the 1970s. Moreover, it was produced from barley malted at the distillery's own floor maltings, distilled on Tuesday, 25 November 1975, and originally filled into two separate casks – a bourbon barrel and an Oloroso sherry hogshead. These casks had aged for 38 years when Dr Lumsden decided to marry the two casks. On 31 March 2014, the whiskies were combined in a single refill Oloroso sherry butt, which had been chosen to contribute the subtlest wood influence.

Dr Lumsden's tasting note includes Brazil nuts and toffee, followed by linseed oil, aromatic peat smoke and a tobacco hint on the nose. The palate combines complexity and elegance, with spearmint top notes, hints of lapsang souchong tea, biscuits and espresso coffee simmering alongside salted caramel and toffee. The finish unites smoke and oak.

Over the next five years, Ardbeg will continue to mature Cask No. 3 in a secure location on Islay on behalf of the owner, who will receive a certain number of bottles from the cask until 2026. This will mean a vertical series of 46, 47, 48, 49 and 50 year old Ardbeg. While £16 million is an enormous amount of money for a cask, this equates to £36,000 per bottle, which is hardly unusual for a malt of this age and such rarity.

Crafting spirit

When a malt is as generous with phenolics as Ardbeg, the peating level is inevitably a focus. This is usually 50 ppm, though experimental batches between 18 and 54 ppm and even 72 ppm have been distilled. The Robert Boby mill was brand new when acquired in 1921, with a milling specification of 70 per cent grits, 20 per cent husk and 10 per cent flour, and having positioned my nose above the flour I can confirm there are definitely phenolic notes present.

The cast iron mash tun has ornamental panels on the exterior, which is the original livery, but now encases a stainless steel mash tun that produces a clear wort.

I had an opportunity to pry into several of the Oregon pine washbacks and compare different stages of fermentation. At 30 hours, numerous small bubbles resembled tiny twinkling lights like a constellation of stars. At 50 hours, when all the action is down to secondary fermentation (yeast autolysis and lactic acid), the heat of the fermentation creates natural currents in the liquid, which propel forward, then change direction, as though looking for a way out.

A sample of wash at 8% abv was acquired using a dunker (a mini-milk churn on a chain) for me to nose. This showed malty, bread notes, then shandy (having the body of beer with the lightness and sweetness of lemonade). 'Oregon pine washbacks also help to establish estery, waxy, carbolic notes in the wash,' says Colin Gordon.

The stillhouse at Ardbeg is significantly larger than its predecessor, accommodating four new stills (the original two remain intact within the previous stillhouse). The original ogee shape was reproduced to promote reflux, and both lyne arms ascend, promoting more reflux.

I couldn't wait to climb the stairs to a mezzanine walkway, which provides a rare opportunity to get up close and personal to the upper sections of the stills. I've always admired the gleaming sheen of copper and symmetrical rivet work, which is a practicality, holding two overlapping sections together, while also having an industrial chic. The rivet work on these stills was a revelation, set within a decorative band of copper that has an 'X' pattern impressed between each rivet. The overall impression is of a supersized Arts and Crafts bracelet ordered from an atelier.

Islay has the highest population of riveted stills, partly because distilleries were regularly mothballed and the stills remained in good condition. Riveting was standard practice until the late 1960s, when welding took over. A riveted seam is very strong, as it is overlapping, but it is also time-consuming to produce, whereas welding is quicker and more practical.

Vapours exiting the stills enter the lyne arms, which ascend at a slight angle and have a purifier attached. This is a feature in its own right, like a matching accessory. Purifiers are rare in Scotland, though Ardbeg is a prime example on Islay. The role of a purifier is to provide a cooler temperature that causes some condensation and creates additional reflux, increasing the proportion of lighter notes and level of sweetness.

'Some vapours are drawn into the purifier from the lyne arm, but the majority is liquid, as it's cooler in the purifier than the lyne arm, and from the purifier the condensate is returned to the pot with a double bend in the pipework between the purifier and the pot, adding further reflux,' Colin explains. 'Without the purifier the spirit character would be chunkier and meatier.'

Experiencing this meatier incarnation is possible thanks to a creative experiment conducted by Dr Bill Lumsden. This involved temporarily 'disabling' the purifier to enable the richest vapours to reach the top of the stills and continue to the condensers. The result was Ardbeg Heavy Vapours, a limited edition released in 2023, which has surging bittersweet notes on the palate, including peppermint and cardamom, before dark chocolate emerges.

When vapours reach the shell and tube condensers, the water coming into the condensers in winter is 4–5°C (39–41°F), and 18–20°C (64–68°F) in summer. The effect of warmer water is condensation occurring lower down in the condenser, which means more copper contact in the vapour phase (which is more intense), and less in the liquid phase (a milder interaction). When the water is colder, vapours condense higher up in the condenser and the vapours have less copper contact, whereas the liquid has more.

These seasonal variations in the new make spirit profile are a fascinating topic. As Colin says: 'The difference will be very slight. The vast majority of copper contact happens in the stills and purifier. By the time the spirit has matured, the differences between winter and summer distillation will not be noticeable, in my view. However, there is no denying the older generation of distillers always preferred the spirit distilled in winter.'

The new make spirit character is 'peaty, smoky, citrus fruit, particularly smoky lime, with herbal notes that continue with liquorice and fennel. New make spirit is around 20–25 ppm; the greatest loss is in the feints,' says Colin.

The distillation process is controlled from a workstation that resembles a reception desk at a boutique hotel. Behind the workstation is a vast window occupying the width of the front elevation. When I arrived at the stillhouse, raindrops had formed patterns on the glass that obscured the view. In the course of my visit, the weather had changed from rain to sunshine (hardly unusual on Islay). The vast window had opened, and was in position like a glass platform at a right angle to the wall of the stillhouse. I was amazed, not expecting such dexterity from a window that is a whopping 8 metres (26 feet) wide and 4 metres (13 feet) high. The view included the pier, where puffers used to dock. Sunlight glittered on the sea, and in the distance I could see the coast of Northern Ireland.

Maturing malt whisky

The filling store occupies part of warehouse No. 9, where the traditional filling strength is 63.7% abv. Why this strength was chosen – rather than the industry standard of 63.5% abv – is unknown. As so often, tradition is honoured and maintained!

'Of the 19,000 casks ageing here, 90 per cent are bourbon barrels from various distilleries in the States. We use a variety of casks, but mainly first and second fill are used for our single malt expressions,' says Colin.

After three years in a first-fill bourbon barrel there is abundant vanilla and coconut, with citrus really showing, together with smoky, salty notes. At 12 years, a first-fill bourbon has plenty of creamy vanilla, Victoria sponge and smoke, which evolve into sticky toffee pudding.

A first-fill Oloroso sherry cask takes Ardbeg in a different direction. Colin observes: 'I always feel the smoke is slightly less prevalent in sherry casks compared to bourbon barrels, but it is there, it is Ardbeg. Dried fruits, especially raisin, is a note I pick up in the 3 year old samples, and we get a lovely smoked meat note in 12 year old Oloroso sherry casks. Tannins are also more noticeable in the 12 year old than the 3 year old.'

The remaining 0.8 per cent of the inventory is sherry butts, typically Oloroso. However, Ardbeg Smoke Trails showcases a Manzanilla influence, a style of sherry known for dry, sea salt notes, which matches Islay's maritime influence. The result is vanilla alongside brine, roasted nuts, fudge and dark chocolate aromas, giftwrapped in barbecue notes with olive brine, hints of olive oil and fried bread.

Ardbeg's ageing warehouses are numbered 3, 9 (dunnage) and 10 and 11 (racked), which may sound eccentric. There was a warehouse no. 1 and nos 4–8, but these were demolished in the 1960s, and the original numbering retained.

The warehouses harbour many forthcoming releases, including exclusives for members of the Ardbeg Committee, which now totals 180,000 members in 140 countries. 'If there's one thing we know about Ardbeggians, it's that they're an eclectic mix of people – whisky mad and up for anything. But they all bond over one shared passion – smoky Ardbeg malt. We look forward to hearing their thoughts on our latest expression. And to anybody not already part of the family, we invite you to join the Ardbeg Committee...and join in the conversation!' says Colin .

Ardbeg tasting notes

Ardbeg 10 year old 46% abv

Nose: Like a soprano filling a concert hall with a sophisticated medley of notes: sea breeze, brine and green olives with a lemon zest garnish adding freshness, then smoke and brioche join in.

Palate: The voice of a tenor, with weight in the mouthfeel: vanilla, toasted, smoke with dark chocolate, green olives and seasalt lusciousness, with olives in brine having the final word.

Finish: Tangy, fruity notes with smoke, oak and a juicy-dry balance.

Ardbeg Uigeadail 54.2% abv

Nose: Arrives rich and focussed on a sea breeze, with brine and green olives that meld into mulled wine with a clove highlight, gently suffused with smoke and roasted nuts.

Palate: Becomes juicy and luscious very quickly, artfully composed with sweetness and smoke opening up, sprinkled with sea salt, which adds lusciousness, then a slice of tortilla. Expands impressively on the palate while retaining order.

Finish: Sweetness and lusciousness are soon underlined by a platform of dryness and oak, and a hint of savoury richness.

Ardbeg Smoke Trails 46% abv

Nose: Bonfire on the beach, with wafting smoke directed by a sea breeze along with roasted nuts and linseed; then turns savoury and fruity, with olives, anchovies and grilled peppers.

Palate: Embracing personality, with roasted nuts and chargrilled notes at the core and smoke permeating the edges; olives and anchovies emerge at the forefront, with subtle top notes of creamy vanilla sprinkled with flakes of sea salt adding lusciousness.

Finish: Light dryness followed by grilled peppers, oak and a hint of sweetness soon yielding to lemon and sea salt.

Ardbeg Lord of the Isles 46% abv

This is a blend of casks filled in 1974–6, released in 2001.

Nose: Crème brûlée, dark chocolate, gingerbread and clove, with wafts of carbolic soap, black olives, and earthy peat coming and going; poised and intriguing.

Palate: Soft mouthfeel, enveloping lusciousness, honey, crème caramel, orange marmalade, salted lemon, toasty, smoky, digestive biscuit notes come and go, with a final waft accompanied by dark chocolate.

Finish: Additional burst of peat with wafts of smoke.

Ardbeg 17 year old 40% abv

Nose: Ripe fruit suffused with smoke, lashings of vanilla custard with a gentle secondary waft of smoke, then orange marmalade and a nutmeg flourish supplemented by digestive biscuits.

Palate: An elegant texture delivers generous vanilla and gingerbread, accompanied by a waft of nutmeg, then salty lemon evolves with sweet oranges providing contrast and complement, with a hint of digestive biscuits.

Finish: Ripe fruit opens up, dryness gradually builds and culminates in a chocolate, malty combination.

Ardbeg 1976 (bottled 2002) 53.1% abv

Nose: Lively oak, linseed and walnuts, seasoned with cloves and ginger and a generous dusting of cocoa powder, then luscious vanilla custard becomes the focal point with big toffee, rich marzipan and Battenberg cake in its wake.

Palate: Animated palate, attractively flamboyant, with salty lemon balanced by dark chocolate and cocoa powder. Fruit trifle opens up with rich marzipan and walnuts, with a background waft of peat. Maintains its indulgent, luscious nature.

Finish: Big dark chocolate notes that extend with toffee and fudge.

Chapter Five

Ardnahoe

Chapter Five

Ardnahoe

En route to Ardnahoe on a December morning, the sun was rising above distant hills, casting a golden light. Opposite the sun, above Loch Indaal, a luminous full moon hung in a clear blue sky. It was a magnificent sight.

The full moon has a particular relationship with Loch Ardnahoe, a deep inland loch that provides the distillery with water. Legend states that moonlight beckons a spirit from the depths of the loch, a magnificent white steed that emerges from the water and walks along the shore. What this excursion means to the steed and why it was consigned to the depths of the loch are unknown, though following the route of the steed provides views across the loch that are difficult to leave behind.

Red deer don't wait for a full moon to emerge from the nearby Sound of Islay, a volatile stretch of seawater dividing Islay from Jura, and stroll along the shores of Islay by the distillery as they please. These are confirmed sightings, as red deer swim from Jura to Islay, a distance of just under a mile. Jura has a population of 7,000 deer (and 200 people), so it's hardly surprising that some red deer occasionally want to get away from the crowd.

Origins

Falling in love can happen anywhere, and at any time. Stewart Hunter Laing fell in love with Islay and Islay malts when he arrived at Bruichladdich distillery in 1963 to learn about distillation. The following year, Stewart joined his father's blending and bottling company in Glasgow, where he developed a blended Scotch called House of Peers, and released single-cask and cask-strength malt whiskies. In 2013, Stewart founded his own blending and bottling company, Hunter Laing & Co., with his sons Andrew as export director and Scott as a director. The portfolio included Scarabus, an Islay single malt, and single malts under the Kinship label including Ardbeg, Bowmore, Bruichladdich, Caol Ila and Laphroaig. But Stewart's dream was to bottle an Islay malt distilled at his own distillery.

A shortlist of five sites was being considered, then one more was suggested near Loch Ardnahoe. And that proved to be the one. In 2016, Stewart acquired the site. Planning permission was granted, and in January 2017 construction work began. As the site sloped down towards the Sound of Islay, this initially meant digging out thousands of tonnes of rock to create a flat area on which to build. Crushing the rock provided a solid foundation and the first concrete slabs were laid in May.

An archive of knowledge, experience and passion joined the team when Jim McEwan was appointed production director of Ardnahoe Distillery in 2017. Jim is an incredible resource, having spent 34 years at Bowmore, followed by 15 years at Bruichladdich and a brief retirement of 18 months. 'I had intended to ride off into the sunset, but I've known Stewart for many years. When I visited the distillery site with the Laing family, it absolutely blew me away,' Jim says. 'It felt as though the stars were aligning; the amazing location, my history with Islay, my relationship with the Laing family, their passion for the project, the calibre of architect Iain Hepburn, plus my chance to get involved with the design of the distillery for the first time in my career, all made it feel like it was 'meant to happen'.'

In September 2017, Speyside Copper Works began welding copper sections of the stills, with steel frames for the buildings assembled in November 2017. In May 2018, two important arrivals included a Vickers Boby mill, dating from 1920 – the only piece of equipment that is not new – sourced by the engineer who services it. (I had to ask where the mill came from, but this is not revealed. Where it is now, is more important than where it was.) Timber for the washbacks was machined by JB Vats in the company's workshop in Dufftown, Speyside, and flat-packed for delivery. On arrival at Ardnahoe the vats were built in situ, and fitted with steel hoops that were made to measure on site.

Pot stills also arrived in sections and were then welded together on-site, but the lyne arms arrived in one piece. The worm tubs were produced by L H Stainless and copper worms arrived already assembled, and were installed in June 2018. Getting connected to the grid wasn't a problem, as electricity was already being supplied to neighbouring Bunnahabhain distillery.

That was the equipment sorted out, and what it needed to achieve was clear.

'The house style was to be a fruit-forward new make spirit, but with robust smoky notes. You can influence the character of the new make spirit and the resulting malt whisky, but you can't 100 per cent engineer the result,' says distillery manager Fraser Hughes.

The first mash was on 9 October 2018, using Concerto peated to 40–45 ppm by Port Ellen Maltings. The first new make spirit ran on 14 October 2018, with Jim McEwan among those present, and as there were no feints, this initially manifested itself with plenty of elegance and sweetness.

Stewart's Islay malt whisky interests have continued to diversify, with Hunter Laing launching Scarabus (meaning 'rocky place') during Fèis Ìle in May 2019. Scarabus Specially Selected is an Islay single malt with peat smoke and sea salt aromas, and in November 2020 a 10 year old was added to the portfolio, together with a more intense option of the 10 year old bottled at the batch strength of 57% abv.

In 2021, the first 3 year old Ardnahoe malt (therefore legally Scotch whisky) was ready to be sampled. 'But there is no date fixed for the inaugural release,' Fraser says. 'It will be released when judged ready.' And that raises the question of what the criteria will be for this. We'll just have to wait and see.

Walking through the distillery, it is beautifully ordered and serene, spacious walkways like viewing galleries linking a series of interconnected function rooms – except that the functions are not social or corporate, but for producing malt whisky. And that, of course, begins with malted barley.

'Sourcing barley was very challenging in 2022. There are only four to five commercial maltsters that can supply peated malt, and demand has increased as more distilleries on the mainland are also using peated malt,' Fraser explains. 'There are also infrastructure issues, for example there isn't a separate ferry for freight. At times there is only one ferry, sometimes two, for freight and passengers with cars, but hopefully a new ferry will be operational in late 2024, early 2025.'

Fraser was born in Inverness, not far from Tomatin Distillery where his father worked, before moving to various other distilleries and being appointed distillery manager at Bowmore in 1979. Fraser also worked at Bowmore, showing visitors around the distillery before becoming a warehouseman in 1985. In 1989, he moved back to the mainland to work at Auchentoshan, then Glen Garioch, where he was appointed distillery manager in 2001. He returned to Islay in 2018 to be part of the team that launched Ardnahoe.

Crafting spirit

Laureate barley has been used since 2020, milled to the usual industry specification: 70 per cent grits, 20 per cent husk and 10 per cent fines, to promote a clear wort. A stainless steel mash tun accessorized with a copper domed lid uses water from Loch Ardnahoe, the objective being the clearest wort possible.

Oregon pine was chosen for the washbacks rather than stainless steel, as heat transfer from the ambient temperature is more immediate with stainless steel than wood. Fermentation lasts 70–75 hours, during which abundant fruit aromas fill the area: apples, pears and even pineapples.

The result is a fruity wash with an alcoholic strength of 8–9% abv. The stillhouse has a wonderful minimalism; the wash and spirit still are in serene alignment and resemble an installation in an art gallery. Beyond the stills, a vast picture window frames a work of art: the magnificent Sound of Islay and the Jura coastline beyond.

The wash still, with a 12,500-litre (2,700-gallon) capacity, produces fruity, low wines around 25–26% abv, not to mention amazing apple and pear aromas filling the stillhouse. The spirit still, with a 9,000-litre (2,000-gallon) capacity, reaches a peak strength of about 74.5% abv before decreasing. Once the heads run clear, the still man can begin nosing samples to monitor the decrease in undesirable 'off-notes' such as aldehydes, which can give earthy, decomposing vegetable notes.

'However, the heads also contain the bulk of the fruit notes, so it's a balancing act where you start collecting. If we let the heads run a bit longer there would be less fruit in the new make spirit,' says Fraser.

The alcoholic strength at which the spirit cut begins and ends is not disclosed, although the profile is. 'The spirit cut goes from lighter to heavier. Pineapple, apples and pears come through, with the bulk of phenolics at the start and end of the spirit cut, with more creosote and tar at the end. We cut to feints just before sweaty, vegetal, burned oil and ash appear in the distillate,' Fraser explains.

Magnificent lyne arms are actually the longest in Scotland, measuring 7.5 metres (25 feet). Such dimensions significantly increase the level of copper contact, and the temperature is that much cooler at the exit than the entrance, creating greater reflux.

From the lyne arm, vapours begin another long journey through a copper worm. This is a different experience for vapours than at any other Islay distillery, as only Ardnahoe has worms. Each worm measures

77 metres (84 yards), configured in concentric decreasing circles as it descends to the base of the worm tub. This is a stainless steel tub, clad in strips of larch purely for aesthetics, holding 35,000 litres (7,700 gallons) of water. Cold water is pumped into the base of the tub at a rate of 1,200 litres (264 gallons) per minute. This water rises, cooling the worm, then exits from the top of the tub, having also been warmed by the heat of the worm (due to the vapours within). Warm water is conducted to a cooling tower, where it drips through a jacket, through which cold air blows. This reduces the temperature of the water droplets so that the water can be returned to the worm tub and repeat the process. Reusing water on a closed-loop system minimizes the amount drawn from Loch Ardnahoe.

The alcoholic strength of the new make spirit is not disclosed, but the profile is. 'The new make spirit has a viscous texture and is fruit-forward, with some sweetness coming through, and drifting but punchy smoke. The peating level is around 25 per cent of the malted barley,' says Fraser.

Some casks are filled at distillation strength, but the majority are filled at the industry standard of 63.5% abv. Initially, several hundred casks were laid down for ageing at the distillery, with a filling store and racked warehouse for up to 20,000 casks added in 2023. Four more ageing warehouses are planned to be up and running by 2030: these will be racked, stacking up to ten casks high, together with smaller dunnage warehouses with slate roofs.

Maturing malt whisky

The first spirit was laid down in November 2018, with 70 per cent of the cask inventory being first-fill bourbon barrels. How a malt whisky develops can, of course, be guided, but when there is no track record there is also an element of wait and see. 'After four years the smoke is there but initially less evident in first-fill bourbon, with light, bright fruit including pineapple more abundant, accompanied by crème brûlée. As the fruit mellows the smoke shows more. The smoke will wane slightly with longer ageing, but we don't know when,' says Fraser.

The cask selection also includes refill bourbon barrels, intended for longer-term ageing (as the influence is mellower than first fill), together with quarter casks, European oak Oloroso and Pedro Ximénez sherry casks, hogsheads and butts. 'Four years in a first-fill Oloroso cask gives a richer flavour than a first-fill Bourbon barrel, with more smoke also coming through. It's a balance of sweet and dry, with orange peel, oranges, plums, prunes, raisins and dates and more tannins. The apple and pear notes you see in our bourbon-aged malt are also there, but not as pronounced,' says Fraser.

Such appetizing descriptors! But I was listening rather than tasting myself. The inevitable question is, when will we get to sample it? 'When it's ready.' Quite right. It must be a creative decision, not a commercial one. I'll just have to wait. Impatiently.

Bowmore

Chapter Six

Bowmore

The first distillery I visited on Islay was Bowmore in 1997, hosted by Jim McEwan, then Bowmore's global brand ambassador. I had met him at a tasting he held in London. We chatted afterwards and I told him my interest in malt whisky had just begun and that I was eager to learn. He invited me to Bowmore, and several weeks later there I was.

Touring the distillery with Jim was fascinating because he explained the technicalities of production, while also hailing the people involved. Having joined Bowmore as an apprentice cooper in 1963, he subsequently worked in every department, from warehousing and cellar master to trainee blender and distillery manager.

Jim also arranged for me to visit Islay's other distilleries during my trip, which at that time included Ardbeg, Bunnahabhain, Caol Ila, Laphroaig and Lagavulin. Jim wanted me to appreciate all of Islay's malt whiskies as well as Bowmore. And I greatly appreciated him.

Origins and expressions

Islay's oldest working distillery, Bowmore was established by an Islay farmer, David Simson, in 1779. However, a famine on Islay led to a ban on distillation in 1782 in an attempt to conserve grain. This was revoked within a couple of years, and was followed by the Wash Act in 1784, which aimed to encourage illicit distillers to take out a licence by making distilling a more profitable venture. Simson's income was boosted by owning a small vessel that brought supplies to Islay, mooring at the town's pier, adjacent to the distillery. Growing profits from distilling meant that Simson was able to spend £65 creating a new watercourse to supply the distillery in 1825.

In 1837, Bowmore was acquired by James and William Mutter, farmers from Dalkeith, near Edinburgh. New kilns arrived, additional ageing warehouses were built and the stillhouse was extended and fitted with a remarkable style of pot still known as a stork-headed still (a traditional still is referred to as having a 'swan neck'). This meant two separate lyne arms extending from the neck of the still to individual worms, and is thought to have been the sole example in the industry. Sadly, there is no record of the influence this had on the new make spirit, and how long they were in service is also uncertain. If the stills had been judged a success, it is very likely that more documentation would have survived.

As production levels grew, larger volumes of water were required, and another new watercourse (known as a 'lade') was established in 1840, drawing on the island's most important river, the Laggan, which continues to be the distillery's water source. However, the land was so flat that the lade had to be carefully planned. Drops of water were applied to a waxed thread stretched along the proposed route, and their progress monitored to ensure it was viable. Although it's less than five miles from the river to the distillery, the lade totalled almost nine miles in length.

A greater distance, between Bowmore distillery and Glasgow, was spanned by the SS *James Mutter*, a 145-tonne iron steamship commissioned by James Mutter. This brought coal to fire the stills and barley from Inverness and Morayshire, while taking casks of malt whisky to the company's warehouses in Glasgow, housed under the arches of the central railway station. An entrepreneur, James Mutter combined co-running Bowmore and owning a couple of farms on Islay, while also appointed honorary vice-consul in Glasgow for the Ottoman Empire, Portugal and Brazil.

By 1880, Bowmore was producing around 200,000 gallons of malt whisky annually, making it the second largest distillery on Islay behind Ardbeg, at 250,000 gallons. This was a successful business for William and James Mutter to hand over to their sons in 1880. However, they did not have their fathers' aptitude for commerce, and after ten years the distillery went into liquidation. In 1892, ownership of Bowmore passed to a London consortium, The Bowmore Distillery Company, and in 1925 it was acquired for £20,000 by J B Sherriff & Co., which already owned the Lochindaal Distillery in nearby Port Charlotte (extinct since 1929).

The outbreak of the Second World War led to the distillery ceasing production in 1940, when taken over by Coastal Command, including 422 Squadron of the Royal Canadian Air Force. Coastal Command operated Catalina and Sunderland flying boats, and one of their tasks was to spot U-boats in the Atlantic.

Post-war expansion included new malt barns in 1948, new malt bins and a boiler in 1949, and no. 5 warehouse completed in 1958. The distillery had by this point been acquired by William Grigor & Son Ltd of Inverness. Bowmore entered a modern era and began developing a more international profile after being acquired in 1963 by a successful whisky brokerage based in Glasgow, Stanley P Morrison Ltd (subsequently Morrison Bowmore Distillers Ltd).

The following year was marked by major changes. Steam-heated coils were introduced to heat the stills, replacing direct coal fire, which can significantly affect the new make spirit character. A new boiler and wash still were ordered and had to be delivered by the Royal Navy. However, the ship arrived earlier than the distillery manager had advised. The tide was so low that the ship was unable to reach the harbour and remained a few hundred yards from the shore. Distillery staff, joined by locals, pulled guy ropes attached to the ship, but this didn't bring it any nearer. Laying caterpillar tracks on the bed of Loch Indaal for trucks to drive across with the equipment didn't work either. After five days the water level rose, the boat inched nearer, the trucks were able to navigate the caterpillar tracks and the cargo reached the shore.

These changes to the distillation regime produced spirit with characteristics that have never been equalled. Whether this was due to the new heating method, the new wash still (offering fresh copper, as well as being a different size and shape to its predecessor) or a combination of factors including an outstanding barley harvest is uncertain. The only certainty is the result: Bowmore from 1964, including the renowned Black Bowmore, has attained an incredible allure and status.

In August 1980, Her Majesty Queen Elizabeth II visited Bowmore, the first whisky distillery the Queen had visited. To mark the occasion, a sherry butt known as the Queen's Cask was filled with new make spirit and placed in no. 1 vault within a specially constructed viewing area.

In 1989, the Japanese conglomerate Suntory acquired a 35 per cent shareholding in Morrison Bowmore. Suntory already owned Japanese whiskies including Yamazaki, Hibiki and Hakushu, while Morrison Bowmore's portfolio included Auchentoshan in the Lowlands and Glen Garioch in the Highlands. In 1994, Suntory purchased the remaining shares in Morrison Bowmore to own the company outright. Meanwhile, a local development saw Morrison Bowmore donate no. 1 warehouse (a separate warehouse from the no. 1 vault) to the community of Islay in 1991. This was repurposed into the Mactaggart Leisure Centre, with a fitness area and swimming pool. The distillery also makes a continuous contribution to the centre by heating water for the swimming pool.

The 1990s saw Bowmore develop a broader portfolio, including the release of malts distilled in 1964 (after new equipment was introduced). These limited editions were known as Black Bowmore, named after the dark hue that ageing in sherry casks produced. The first release in 1993 comprised 2,000 bottles of a 29 year old. In 1994, another 2,000 bottles of a 30 year old followed, with 1,812 bottles of a 31 year old released in 1995. The initial price of £110 per bottle has risen dramatically. For collectors, it's preferable – even imperative – to own a set of all three. A

Black Bowmore Trilogy sold for £93,750 when auctioned by Bonhams in December 2018.

Longer-aged malts were rare in the 1990s, and the release of Bowmore 40 year old in 1995 was a pinnacle, with each of the 306 bottles retailing at £4,000. The same year saw Bowmore's first special finish launched with Bowmore Darkest Sherry Casked, adding the influence of Oloroso sherry butts during a finishing period to malt matured in bourbon barrels. In 2000, Bowmore Dusk Bordeaux Wine Casked saw malts aged for at least 12 years in bourbon and sherry casks subsequently filled into claret casks for a two-year finishing period. This added abundant redcurrants, wild cherries, rosehip syrup, raspberries and damsons, with a creamy sherbet emerging mid-palate.

Another celebration that year was provided by a new world record auction price for a bottle of malt, established at McTear's auction rooms in Glasgow. A Bowmore 1890, believed to be one of the last bottlings under the Mutter family, and personally engraved for James Mutter, achieved £14,300.

In 2002, the year of the Queen's Golden Jubilee, the Queen's Cask had reached 21 years of age. After discussions with Buckingham Palace, it was bottled to celebrate the Golden Jubilee, with the cask yielding 648 bottles hand-filled at the distillery at a cask strength of 51.1% abv. Her Majesty was presented with the entire bottling to give as gifts to foreign dignitaries and guests at Buckingham Palace. The Palace also granted that one bottle be permanently displayed at Bowmore distillery.

Among Bowmore's illustrious bottlings, one particular vintage has a superlative status: 1964. This was an amazing year for Bowmore. Was it because of the new pot stills installed that year, the cask selection, the barley? Who knows. But the result was evident in 2002–3 when the first three vintages distilled in 1964 were released, each showcasing a different cask influence. Bowmore Fino Cask was released in autumn 2002, the Oloroso Cask followed in spring 2003, with the Bourbon Cask released in autumn 2003. Further bottlings of the celebrated 1964

vintage were released in 2002, with 300 bottles of the 1964 Fino Sherry Cask at £1,000 each. In 2003, a trio of 1964 bottlings was launched: a Bourbon Cask, a Fino Cask (Fino being a dry style of sherry) and Oloroso Cask (a richer style of sherry). I was fortunate enough to experience this trio, at a special tasting held at the Stafford Hotel in St James's, London (my tasting notes are included on pages 116–7).

In 2012, Bowmore released a 54 year old, the oldest Islay ever, distilled in 1957 and priced at £100,000 per bottle. This was also the year that David Turner was appointed distillery manager. David had passed the distillery every day on his way from Port Ellen to his school in Bowmore, and he joined Bowmore distillery in 1990 straight from school, when the distillery manager was his mother's cousin's husband, and his grandfather had also worked at Bowmore.

David started in the ageing warehouses, then moved on to the malt barns. 'I was immediately fascinated by the ageing warehouses, and the process in the malt barns, where the process is subject to so many variables,' he says. 'There was a great camaraderie, and the guys were so experienced and passed on to me what they had learned from the previous generation.'

Working in a distillery is a job for life for many employees, and it doesn't end then either. 'Retired guys still come into the distillery to say hello, and if I see them in the street they ask me what's happening on the malt floors,' says David.

Crafting spirit

As one of the few distilleries to operate floor maltings, the steeping regime means filling the stainless steel steeps with barley (Laureate replaced Concerto in 2021), and water from the River Laggan. Once it reaches a moisture level of 42–44 per cent, the barley is transported to the malting floor in traditional wooden chariots (barrows). Two steeps provide 14 tonnes of malt, which covers one malting floor (there are three malting floors in total).

Barley is spread across the floors at a consistent depth of several inches, to promote uniform growth as the barley germinates. It takes about nine hours in summer and twelve hours in winter for the chit (rootlet) to appear. This is the sign to start turning (aerating) the barley. Malt shiels (wooden spades) and a rake (resembling a small plough) that malt men drag behind them are used to turn the malt every four hours, around the clock. The shifts are 10.00 a.m.–6.00 p.m., 6.00 p.m.–2.00 a.m. and 2.00 a.m.–10.00 a.m.

New recruits at Bowmore always start on the malting floor. I tried raking – not that I'd been recruited, I just wanted to know how it felt. It's hard work. And I didn't rake for long. A real malt man can rake the entire floor in around 35 minutes, and each time the floor is raked the direction of travel changes from north-south to east–west for more thorough aeration (which is confirmed by the 'grid' pattern created on the bed).

The grain reaches optimum growth after seven days, and is then ready for kilning. Malt is spread across the perforated floor of the kiln to form a bed about 30 cm (1ft) deep. A fire in the kiln is started with wood shavings, then slowly covered with 'bricks' of peat arranged like a tipi. Peat is cut from the Glenmachrie peat bank near the distillery, and contains abundant seaweed, sphagnum moss, heather, pine needles and grasses, with a slightly oily texture.

Small batches of Bowmore's floor-malted barley are distilled and aged separately, with ongoing trials exploring different barley varieties and specifications. Meanwhile, production means a combination of floor-malted and commercially malted barley: every 2 tonnes of Bowmore's malted barley is blended with 6 tonnes of malt from Simpsons Malt.

Water for mashing is sourced from the River Laggan and heated in two 'coppers': magnificent spherical copper vessels that are a rarity in Scotland. Dating from 1938, the coppers were originally coal-fired; the current steam coils were fitted within the coppers in 1963.

Seven Oregon pine washbacks all have the same 40,000-litre (8,800-gallon) capacity but an individual identity, as each one is named after a previous owner of the distillery, for example James and William Mutter. Oregon pine replaced stainless steel washbacks in 1990, which had in turn replaced wooden washbacks in 1964. The reason for returning to wood was the fruitier profile this promotes.

Fermentation is 62 hours (which was set 20 years ago), producing a wash with fruity green apple and banana alongside phenolics, at a strength of around 8% abv.

One condenser is on the exterior of the stillhouse, and the other on the interior where the ambient temperature is higher. This promotes a slightly longer vapour phase, and consequently slightly lighter, fruitier spirit, though distillate from both condensers is combined. 'In the new make spirit we're looking for floral, orchard fruit, green grass, cereal and medicinal, leathery notes,' says David Turner, Bowmore's distillery manager.

A small batch of Bowmore's floor-malted barley was first distilled as a separate parcel in 2016, and has subsequently been an annual event. These parcels are still in the ageing warehouses, so how they mature remains to be seen. However, one indication is that floor-malted new make spirit is a bit fruitier, richer, rounder and more intense than commercially malted.

Maturing malt whisky

Bourbon barrels supplied by Jim Beam account for the majority of the casks. Sherry casks include Oloroso and Pedro Ximénez. 'Ageing in bourbon barrels shows phenolics most clearly; vanilla and smoke is a nice combination. Pedro Ximénez casks give a sweeter whisky, and phenols tend to come through in the finish,' says David.

A series showing the influence of port casks also features an Islay myth, with The Changeling 22 year old finished in a white port cask, while The Changeling 33 year old is finished in a tawny port cask. Themed bottle labels were created by Frank Quitely, an illustrator from Glasgow whose work has appeared in Marvel and DC Comics. The Changeling is the tale of a blacksmith whose son lay dying. The father was distraught, but a stranger arrived and told him this was a changeling, not his son, his son having been abducted by Islay fairies. The stranger told the blacksmith where to find his son and what to do when he got there. The blacksmith was also given a knife and cockerel; the knife was to prise open a split in Fairy Hill within which his son was incarcerated. This hill is on the south coast overlooking Ardilistry Bay. Deep within the hill was a forge where the son was forced to work, bound by a spell the fairies had cast upon him. The fairies were horrified to see the father appear and refused to give him his son back. This is when the cockerel sprang into action, and it soon became clear why the blacksmith had received it. Spreading its wings, the cockerel crowed loudly and repeatedly until the fairies relented and broke the spell. The blacksmith grabbed his son, they escaped from the hill and lived and worked together at the family forge happily ever after.

No. 1 vault is Scotland's oldest ageing warehouse, dating from 1779, with thick stone walls, but no windows or ventilation; opening the door is the only way for air to enter and exit. The temperature is remarkably stable at 6–8°C (43–46°F) all year. During the winter, Loch Indaal laps against the seafront wall, though the low tides of summer don't quite get there.

I toured the warehouse with David. Inhaling deeply when I stepped through the door, my usual ritual to connect with a warehouse, I was rewarded with a wonderful earthy aroma garnished with Stilton and olive brine. Casks are stacked two high; three is usual in a dunnage, but a low ceiling prevents any more. A wonderful sight was three mizunara (Japanese oak) casks from Yamazaki side by side, filled with Bowmore 20 year old in 2012 and still maturing (mizunara is renowned for taking longer to get results).

Tasting in such a distinguished ageing warehouse is an ultimate experience. David took a valinch and obtained samples straight from casks in the tasting area. A 2003 Bowmore had lovely vanilla creaminess with some biscuit notes, while a 2001 Oloroso sherry cask yielded distinct maritime notes with a hint of sea salt that escalated in the finish.

The influence of the microclimate in this warehouse was expressed in a limited-edition bottling, No. 1 Vault Atlantic Sea Salt, released in 2016.

'Maritime notes don't appear in the new make spirit, you start to notice it after 5 to 7 years, and more so when ageing in bourbon barrels than sherry casks. I would say it's more the sea air than the peat that gives this note, as the casks take in the air,' says David.

Ageing also has a significant effect on the phenolics. 'From our regular range, a 12 year old shows the phenolics most, and it's more on the nose, but peat is never at the forefront of Bowmore. Smoke starts to sit back around 20 years of ageing; it's a gentler version, plus ripe citrus notes turn to tropical fruit,' says David. 'And in our oldest expressions such as a 50 year old, there is oaky, wood smoke in the background and more in the finish than on the nose or palate, with bags of tropical fruit. It's a mellower version of what you would get in a younger malt, though still typically Bowmore.'

Bowmore tasting notes

Bowmore 12 year old 40% abv

Nose: Distinct oak, toasted wood and embers, then a hint of linseed, which is a turning point, ushering in other top notes, vanilla and apricot jam.

Palate: Indulgent vanilla custard, creamy fruit trifle, with underlying toasted notes and gentle wafts of smoke, roasted nuts, then fruit opens up and becomes more luscious with apricots, juicy sweet oranges and burned, buttered toast spread with orange marmalade.

Finish: Sweet, juicy oranges and dry toast appear simultaneously but separately, then meld together giving orange marmalade richness.

Bowmore 18 year old 43% abv

Nose: Fruit dipped in caramel, then zinging grapefruit, chocolate eclair and a hint of walnuts, with grapefruit remaining in the spotlight.

Palate: Lightly silky, creamy mouthfeel, gentle grapefruit hovers, introducing itself, then expands dynamically across the palate, underlined by subtle toasted notes and tiramisu, before more fresh, juicy grapefruit reasserts itself.

Finish: Grapefruit freshness, with richness of lemon bonbons, then dryness joins in, nuttiness makes a subtle gesture, then grapefruit takes over.

Black Bowmore 1964 Cask No. 3709, cask strength 42.1% abv,

Limited edition of 99 bottles from a single Oloroso hogshead cask, aged 35 years in no. 1 vault, released in 2000.

Nose: Medicinal overture, cold stewed tea, floral, jasmine hints, barley sugar, hint of treacle, lightly smoky, hint of coal, peat, sea breezes, marzipan, raisins and roasted malt.

Palate: Rich balanced by fresh citrus acidity, hint of barley sugar, liquorice, treacle, tiny medicinal note, dry cooked fruit, apricot, rich sherry trifle, banana, rosehip syrup and maltiness.

Finish: Remarkably rich and sustained.

Bowmore 1964 Bourbon Barrel, cask strength 43.2% abv

300 bottles released.

Nose: Tremendous, luscious grapefruit, lemon, with wonderfully mellow, lightly earthy peaty waft, touch of bitter orange skin, supple honey and vanilla oakiness providing great structure, hints of jasmine tea, sea spray with a hint of sea air, brine adding a savoury touch.

Palate: Wonderfully luscious with underlying balancing dryness, lightly earthy peatiness extends with grapefruit, luscious lemon, Fino sherry at the edges with a biscuity maltiness emerging, a touch of fresh sea spray adds seasoning, a touch of lemon curd, jasmine tea and supple tannins, dry but animated.

Finish: Elegant with lightly earthy, Fino and lemon notes, very long and sustained dryness.

Bowmore 1964 Fino Cask, cask strength 49.6% abv

Two Fino casks originally contained sherry from Macharnudo, renowned as one of the sherry region's finest vineyard districts, reflecting its chalky white albariza soil. Marrying the two casks yielded 300 bottles.

Nose: Tremendous, luscious grapefruit and lemon, with a mellow, lightly earthy peaty waft, hint of bitter orange zest, honey and vanilla oakiness, hint of jasmine tea, with sea spray and brine adding a savoury touch.

Palate: Wonderfully luscious with underlying balancing dryness, lightly earthy peat extending with grapefruit and lemon, garnished with Fino sherry notes with a malty, biscuity note emerging, seasoned by a touch of sea spray, lemon curd, jasmine tea and supple tannins.

Finish: Elegant and balanced with lightly earthy, Fino sherry and lemon notes, with balancing dryness.

Bowmore 15 year old 43% abv

Nose: Fresh, lightly perfumed prunes and apricots threaded onto a skewer of charred wood, drizzled with caramel.

Palate: Mellow but definite mouthfeel, opens with a fruit and phenolic double act; sweetness grows adding apricot and prune lusciousness, with a refined sweetness at the edges of the palate, and smouldering oak at the base.

Finish: Mellow mix of poached and dried fruit in syrup, burned toast, then malty, digestive biscuits.

Chapter Seven

Bunnahabhain

Chapter Seven

Bunnahabhain

Standing on the terrace of the visitor centre I watched swans floating gracefully in the sea just below, turning their heads and studying the view. They weren't lost, as they know exactly where to go for freshwater, and it's not very far, as the Margadale River flows into the sea nearby. This river is a water source for Bunnahabhain (pronounced *Bunn-na-har-vun*), the name meaning 'mouth of the river' in Gaelic.

Freshwater is, of course, a prime requirement for a distillery, but seawater also provided a vital asset for Bunnahabhain, enabling puffers to moor at the pier to unload barley, yeast and empty casks, and to take casks of malt whisky back to Glasgow. Standing on the pier where the boat used to moor, the coast of Jura is close and clear, though rapid currents surge between Islay and Jura. Further into the distance, across a more serene seascape, Mull is visible in the form of an alluring outline.

Origins and expressions

The origins of Bunnahabhain lie in Fife, where William Alexander Robertson was born in 1833. He moved to Glasgow and began a career in which he picked good business partners. In 1856, he formed a wine and spirit business with Robert Thomson, and they became agents for Fettercairn and Greenock distilleries. In 1860, Robertson went into business with John W Baxter, and Robertson & Baxter was soon established as Glasgow's principal wine and spirit agent, subsequently opening another branch in Leith, Edinburgh. The next step was to open a distillery, and Islay was the venue. Yet again, Robertson found the right partner: William Ford & Sons of Leith, a tea, wine and spirit merchant. Together they created the Islay Distillery Company with a share capital of £32,000. A site was selected on the Sound of Islay, close to the Margadale River. Why such a remote location was chosen is unclear, particularly as it would be reliant on puffers to deliver supplies and collect malt whisky, and the adjacent Sound of Islay was notorious for ocean currents reaching a speed of up to 10 knots in tidal water. However, Bunnahabhain Bay is relatively calm.

Building work began in 1881, with the stone quarried to create space for the distillery also used to construct the buildings. In January 1883, building work was completed and the distillery was operational, with production projected at 200,000 gallons a year. Supplies were delivered to the pier by puffers bringing 900 tonnes of barley at a time; access by ship was better than by the single-track road behind the distillery. In 1887, a recession led Robertson to find another partner, which turned out to be William Grant & Co., the owners of Glenrothes distillery. However, Bunnahabhain's production was used as an ingredient in blended Scotch, rather than bottled as a single malt.

In 1930, the distillery closed due to decreased demand for blends, and the Great Depression, but as the economy recovered and optimism grew, Bunnahbhain reopened in 1937. Production continued to cater for blended Scotch such as Famous Grouse, which used heavily peated Bunnahabhain until the 1960s. With demand for Scotch whisky escalating, the malting floors were closed and a second set of stills was added in 1963 to increase production. This was almost entirely used for blended Scotch, until a change of ownership meant the main customer was Cutty Sark, which required unpeated malt.

It wasn't until 1979 that Bunnahabhain 12 year old was launched as a single malt, which continued to leave the distillery by boat, until the last boat docked at the pier in 1993. From then on, a four-mile single-track road that led from the nearest two-lane road was used.

Burn Stewart acquired Bunnahabhain in 2003, and in 2006 relaunched the 12, 18 and 25 year old with new packaging. In 2010, it was decided to stop chill-filtering and adding caramel colouring (to ensure a consistent colour from batch to batch) and to bottle at 46.3% abv. Four years later, Bunnahabhain was acquired by Distell, a South African drinks company that also owns Three Ships and Bain's Cape Mountain South African Whisky.

The oldest proprietary bottling of Bunnahabhain set a record in 2019, when the online platform Whisky Auctioneer hosted the Scotch Whisky Industry Charity Auction in aid of Beatson Cancer Charity. A Bunnahabhain 50 year old Beatson Sherry Cask No.1 of 1, donated by Distell, raised £12,650 (including buyer commission), which was £7,000 more than the previous auction record for an official Bunnahabhain bottling (and this record still stands).

On 24 March 2020, the Covid-19 lockdown was announced in Scotland. Bunnahabhain's visitor centre had been ready to open on 30 March that year but couldn't, although production continued. The visitor centre and shop was finally able to open in August 2022.

The distillery manager, Andrew Brown, joined Bunnahabhain in 1988. Looking for a job after finishing school on Islay, his then-girlfriend's father (subsequently father-in-law) was Bunnahabhain's still man and secured him a few days' work unloading malt delivered from the mainland by boat, which moored at the pier by the distillery. Andrew then applied for a job at the distillery, but someone else got it, and soon afterwards Andrew was hired by a golf club. Then he got a call from Bunnahabhain. Was he still interested in the job he had applied for, as the person who'd been appointed had failed the medical (then standard for distillery employees). Andrew passed the medical and started in

Bunnahabhain's ageing warehouse, then moved to the mash house and stillhouse, then became assistant team leader, deputizing when the distillery manager was away. In 2010, he was appointed team leader, and distillery manager in 2011.

Crafting spirit

Bunnahabhain produces two expressions: Bunnahabhain is unpeated and accounts for 90 per cent of annual production, while Moine (meaning 'smoke') is peated to 40 ppm and accounts for the remaining 10 per cent. Peated spirit has been produced annually since 2003; prior to that, small batches of experimental peated spirit were distilled in 1997, and very lightly peated spirit in 1991.

The Porteus mill produces a standard specification of 70 per cent grits, 20 per cent husk and 10 per cent fines ready for mashing. And what a mash tun! Having a 15-tonne capacity qualifies this as the largest mash tun on Islay, though operating on this scale can put a lot of strain on the rake, and the amount of grist was reduced to 8.2 tonnes in 2022. Installed in the early 2000s, this stainless steel vessel replaced a cast iron mash tun, as it had developed cracks. The copper lid was already present, a result of modernization carried out in 1963. An unusual feature is a small 'sliding door' on runners that opens to provide a view of the interior (the norm is a porthole-style window that reveals the interior).

Six Oregon pine washbacks host two different yeast strains, Quest MX and Lallemand, used individually since 2022, and the results monitored to see how each yeast behaves in each season of the year and at different ambient temperatures.

When production was five days a week, fermentation times varied: 54 hours during the week and 110 hours over the weekend, with the profile of the resulting wash resembling beer at 56 hours, then moving towards lager and finally to an acidic, dry cider at the end of a long fermentation. When production moved to seven days a week in 2021, the fermentation time was set at 54 hours with the wash typically 8% abv.

Each washback fills two wash stills, and there's plenty to fill, as the wash stills stand 7.3 metres (24 feet) high, and the spirit stills 6.4 metres (21 feet), making them the tallest on Islay.

Long lyne arms (without any gradient) lead to the shell and tube condensers. The journey to the condensers may be the same, but the destination varies, as no. 1 wash and spirit stills have condensers on the exterior of the stillhouse. No. 2 wash and spirit stills, added when the distillery was modernized in 1963, have condensers within the stillhouse. Why this was decided is uncertain. But one certainty is that the ambient temperature experienced by the interior condensers is warmer in winter and hotter in summer. Consequently, vapours condense more gradually in the interior condensers, and experience longer interaction with copper, promoting a slightly lighter, fruitier spirit.

New make spirit from each pair of stills is conducted to a separate receiver, but subsequently combined.

'Unpeated new make spirit shows fruit first, pear drops and green apples, then cereal, malty notes with a tiny hint of oiliness and a robust texture. Some people think there is a tiny phenolic hint, but this is not the case,' says Brendan McCarron, master distiller at Distell (which owns Bunnahabhain).

It's tempting to think that peated spirit is the same as unpeated plus the phenolics, but any differences also alter the balance and the way other characteristics show. 'Peated new make spirit character is smoky, salty, medicinal, with pear drops and green apples clouded in smoke. As it matures, the smoke drops down and green apple and pear and floral notes come through. Saltiness undoubtedly comes from the peat,' Brendan adds.

Maturing malt whisky

The alcoholic strength at which new make spirit is filled into casks was 63.5% abv (the industry standard) until August 2021, when it increased to 65% abv, followed by another increase to 69% abv in 2022. Filling at higher strengths means fewer casks and less warehouse space are needed. And until more warehousing is added, higher filling strengths enable as much stock as possible to be aged on Islay, with all Bunnahabhain and Moine single malt being aged on Islay.

Bunnahabhain's open day during Fèis Ìle has showcased a wide range of finishes, resulting from a secondary ageing period in a particular cask, which adds a specific range of flavours. For Fèis Ìle 2020, Moine Madeira Cask Finish spent three years in Madeira casks, which added figs, vanilla and cinnamon to the palate, with a total of 1,164 bottles. In 2021, Moine Bordeaux Finish produced a combination of smoke, dark grapes and cocoa.

In 2022, two special finishes included Moine Tokaji, which saw mature peated malt spend a year in a Tokaji cask (a renowned Hungarian dessert wine), resulting in smoke and sweetness, white chocolate and citrus. A 1998 Calvados Finish (apple brandy produced in Normandy) combined sweetness with green apples and pears, then indulgent toffee.

The warehouses are of the same construction and many neighbour each other, so conditions are very similar. One exception is warehouse no. 9, which was created in 2010 from the original floor maltings, and that also hosts tastings of malt whisky drawn directly from casks displayed in the tasting area. The selection varies, but when I visited the line-up included an Amarone, Manzanilla sherry and a Moscatel wine cask each containing Bunnahahbhain (unpeated), with an Oloroso sherry hogshead containing Moine (peated).

Warehouse no. 9 inspired the launch of a cask-strength edition of Bunnahabhain 12 year old aged in Oloroso casks. The inaugural edition was bottled in 2021 at 55.1% abv; the second edition in 2022 was 56.6% abv with a palate that included orange marmalade, dried fruits and toasted oak (further editions will follow annually).

'Not all whiskies work at cask strength and many whiskies don't stand up to full maturation in sherry casks. Bottling our 12 year old at cask strength intensifies the core characteristics of spice, cracked black pepper and cinnamon, but not at the expense of our spirit's character. In fact, it enhances it. The mouthfeel and texture of the whisky increases and it shows off the balance of the spirit and the wood, but in a more concentrated form,' says Brendan.

Whether and to what extent sea air influences the profile of Bunnahabhain and Moine during the ageing process is an inevitable question. Peated new make spirit already has a salty tang, but could this be enhanced by sea air? One way of answering – or at least addressing – this question is tracking the progress of unpeated Bunnahabhain. 'The 12, 18 and 25 year old unpeated have some saltiness,' says Brendan. 'There's something about distilling by the sea, something in the air that gets into the distillate; there is definitely salinity in the unpeated malt, and saltiness also comes with time.'

Bunnahabhain tasting notes

Bunnahabhain 12 year old 46.3% abv

Nose: Brioche, chocolate eclair and toffee, then digestive biscuits and cappuccino sprinkled with cocoa powder, with some apricots in the background vying for attention.

Palate: Mouthfeel has good weight, biscuit and biscotti notes provide a brief prequel to rich fruit, with sweet, juicy oranges, creamy fruit trifle and hints of creamy porridge with honey, and a baseline of dry oak.

Finish: A moment of maltiness is followed by fruit cake with glacé cherries, then digestive biscuits and dry oak.

Bunnahabhain 12 year old, cask strength 2022 56.6% abv

Nose: Bold and assured, chocolate, hazelnuts and nougat, then becomes richer with apple tart, raisins and honey.

Palate: Elegant mouthfeel delivers intense but elegant sweetness that soon extends into richness, apricot Danish pastry, apple crumble, raisins, prunes in syrup, baked apples and roasted nuts.

Finish: Prunes, raisins and chocolate eclair, then rich fruit syrup balanced by forthright dryness.

Bunnahabhain Stiuireadair 46.3% abv

Nose: Toffee apples and crème brûlée, then baked apples join in, garnished by lightly toasted notes and oak.

Palate: Very delicate, lightly creamy mouthfeel, equally elegant flavours with balanced sweetness-richness, then citrus notes emerge with a hint of vanilla, then lemon zest adds freshness and focus, with creaminess continuing.

Finish: Very light dryness, extends with creaminess.

Bunnahabhain Ceobanach 46.3% abv

Nose: A medley of toast, smoke and embers, followed by spice and oak, then oak continues alone.

Palate: Elegant mouthfeel yields toasted notes that are joined by earthiness, the texture becomes lightly creamy, then opens up with apricots and vanilla adding sweetness and richness, while oak adds a counterpoint.

Finish: Light dryness opens up but soon softens, then extends with rounder oak notes.

Bunnahabhain 2004 Manzanilla 56.5% abv

Nose: A sequence of individual notes with equal weight: rich, ripe peaches, apricot Danish pastry, pain au chocolat and Brazil nuts, underlined by oak.

Palate: Cream cakes and raisins, moving to fruit cake and chocolate brownie, then chocolate truffles and honey take centre stage, with digestive biscuits, chocolate and cinnamon waiting in the wings. Rich and rewarding.

Finish: Cinnamon, mulled wine, then digestive biscuits and flapjacks.

Bunnahabhain 1966 46.1% abv

Nose: Intense, focussed, fresh, rich and majestic, dried fruit and rich walnuts, with integrated vanilla pod wafting forth, rich, dried citrus zest, chocolate and latte coffee.

Palate: Luscious and rich with ripe, dried fruit, but poised, balanced and with underlying dryness, citrus, lemon zest freshness; lovely, nutty fruit cake, butterscotch and creamy fudge, supporting oaky notes with a hint of tannin adding structure and range, extending with espresso, dark chocolate, cappuccino dusted with cocoa powder, nutmeg and vanilla.

Finish: Rich but clean, with freshness, chocolate and maltiness.

Chapter Eight

Bruichladdich

Chapter Eight

Bruichladdich

Do you believe in destiny? When Jim McEwan was Bowmore's global brand ambassador, he could look across Loch Indaal and see Bruichladdich. The distillery was then closed, and the loch stood between them. But in the year 2000 he played an instrumental role in Bruichladdich reopening, and was master distiller there until 2015.

Adam Hannett grew up on Islay, and the school bus took him past Bruichladdich distillery twice a day. The entrance gates were closed: chained and padlocked together, as it was then mothballed. Adam is now Bruichladdich's head distiller. A case of destiny foretold? I think so.

Origins and expressions

In 1881, three brothers – Robert, William and John Harvey – decided to open a distillery on Islay. They already owned two distilleries, Yoker and Dundas Hill, in their home town of Glasgow, inherited from their father, William Harvey, when he died in 1862. Yoker had originally been acquired by their grandfather, John Harvey, in 1770, who also established Dundas Hill in the same year.

The brothers were a perfect combination: Robert was an engineer, John a distiller, William a financier. Being brothers, everything was agreed on a handshake rather than a contract. That also meant that when there were disagreements there was no contract to refer to. Robert, the youngest, died in 1892, and William gained his brother's shares, making him the majority owner of Bruichladdich (pronounced *Brook-laddie*). William continued to run the distillery until it was mothballed in 1930, and he died in 1937.

Another trio of whisky brothers (rather than blood brothers) – wine merchants Mark Reynier and Simon Coughlin, together with Jim McEwan at Bowmore – united at the end of the 1990s in a bid to purchase the distillery. This was a turbulent decade for Bruichladdich, which had been mothballed in 1994 by then owner Whyte & Mackay. It was acquired that same year by Jim Beam, but mothballed again in 1995. Mark, Simon and Jim's bid was not accepted until Jim Beam was acquired by Fortune Brands. Then Bruichladdich was sold to them for £6.5 million, which included 6,500 casks in the ageing warehouses and all the original equipment. The six employees who had been made redundant by Jim Beam returned to work at the distillery.

The first new make spirit flowed at 8.26 a.m. on 26 May 2001, using peated malt at 40 ppm supplied by Port Ellen Maltings. A bottling hall was installed in 2003, and Islay barley was first cultivated for Bruichladdich in 2004 thanks to an Islay farmer, Raymond Stuart. Once the harvest was gathered in, other Islay farmers could see that growing barley on Islay was possible and the amount of barley cultivated continued to increase. Bere barley (a historic variety) was grown on Islay in 2006–7, but as this variety has a long straw, and Islay has strong winds, it's not suited to the island, and is sourced instead from Orkney.

To mark the reopening of the distillery, Jim McEwan hosted a presentation in London for journalists in 2001. It was exciting to hear plans for the distillery, and the tasting that followed included the Bruichladdich 1986 Valinch 15 year old, matured in an Oloroso sherry cask and bottled at the cask strength of 54.5% abv. I still remember this vividly: it was one of the most magnificent malt whiskies I have ever tasted. Elegance and intensity, subtlety and flamboyance, nuances and singularity (I've included my tasting note on page 143). The original retail price in 2001 was £50 for a 50 cl bottle. This was available in person at the distillery, where you could fill your own bottle to mark the reopening of the distillery.

The first organic malt whisky (unpeated) was distilled in 2003; Mid Coul Farms near Inverness supplied the first batch of organic barley. This was released in 2009, with the same farm providing barley for The Organic 2011 distilled that year. The first biodynamic barley was distilled in 2011, the barley having been harvested the previous year at Yatesbury House Farm in England. At that time there were no biodynamic farms in Scotland. Certified by the UK Biodynamic Association, the principles of biodynamic farming are organic methods that also enhance and regenerate the soil, while also embodying social responsibility, and a business model based on moral principles.

A new era for the distillery began in 2012, when Bruichladdich was purchased by luxury spirits company Rémy Cointreau (which also owns Rémy Martin Cognac, Cointreau and Westland Distillery, a pioneering and innovative whisky distillery in the USA). This greatly increased the resources of the distillery, while retaining autonomy.

A new era began for Adam Hannett in 2015 when he was appointed head distiller, having been at Bruichladdich for 18 years. He started as a tour guide, attracted by Bruichladdich's maverick appeal. 'I fell in love with Bruichladdich, as I could see that it was thinking differently,' Adam says. 'Then I trained as a warehouseman, the mash man, then learned the still with Allan Logan, then assistant manager and then head distiller.'

The distillery expanded significantly in 2018, not in terms of production but in agricultural possibilities, by acquiring Shore House Croft. This comprises 12 hectares (30 acres) of land that neighbours the distillery, and is an R&D (research and development) opportunity, where test plots have been planted with various barley varieties since 2020, and other parcels of land have been drained and grazed by sheep, to prepare the soil for planting.

The amount of barley grown on Islay for Bruichladdich by 22 farmers was 44 per cent of the total requirement in 2022. The 2023 figure is 30 per cent, which doesn't mean less barley overall; it just reflects the increase in production levels. Barley from different farms is combined for Bruichladdich and Port Charlotte expressions, but Octomore is distilled exclusively from barley grown on Octomore Farm (the bottle labels stipulate the farm). The barley from a select number of individual farms is kept aside, designated to be a single-farm origin. Barley from other farms is combined to meet the minimum amount of barley required for it to be malted by Bruichladdich's malting partner, Baird's Malt, in Inverness. This combined harvest is spread across all three single-malt brands including Bruichladdich, Port Charlotte and Octomore.

Crafting spirit

When Bruichladdich emerged from the silent period of 1994–2001, all the original equipment was still present, rather like buying a stately home that's fully furnished. After renovation, the distillery went into production, which meant three styles of new make spirit: Bruichladdich is unpeated, Port Charlotte uses malt peated to 40 ppm, while malt for Octomore is 80 ppm.

Peated Bruichladdich represented a return to tradition, as this had been the house style until 1960 when the peating level was greatly reduced to cater for the American market, where the preference was for low or no peating. Meanwhile, Bruichladdich is also constructing floor maltings on site, due to be operational within the next few years.

Another tradition that has been continued is the lack of computerization, which in some distilleries can run the entire process. Control panels reveal what is happening, but making something happen is a manual operation, with all the data recorded by hand. Admittedly, it's a ballpoint pen and preprinted pages in a binder, rather than an ink pen and leather-bound ledger, but the principle remains. There aren't any training manuals for staff training; this is learned from more experienced colleagues.

The mill dates from 1881, although the colour is more recent. The classic Boby green has been made over and painted Bruichladdich blue, producing a spec of 30 per cent husk, 10 per cent flour and 60 per cent grits for each expression. The cast iron mash tun is another original resident, with decorative panels exemplifying the Victorian belief that even functional equipment should have an aesthetic. However, this mash tun wasn't intended for Bruichladdich, having been commissioned by Bunnahabhain. But when the mash tun arrived on Islay, Bunnahabhain wasn't quite ready to receive it, though Bruichladdich was, so an agreement was reached. And when the mash tun that Bruichladdich had commissioned arrived, it went to Bunnahabhain.

The use of Mauri yeast adds some fleshy fruit flavours and floral notes, lilac and roses, which are more prominent as a result of being fermented in wooden washbacks rather than stainless steel. Longer fermentation increases the fruit notes in Port Charlotte and Bruichladdich, and Bruichladdich also has stronger malt notes than Port Charlotte or Octomore. All three expressions gain slightly more vanilla notes (derived from the barley) in a longer fermentation. The resulting wash is 8% abv, with no difference in the yield of alcohol from shorter (72 hours) or longer fermentation (100 hours), or from peated and unpeated malt, though mainland barley gives higher yields than Islay barley.

The absence of computerization in the stillhouse means every decision rests on the still man. When to go from heads to the spirit cut means taking samples of distillate and mixing them 50/50 with spring water. When clear (rather than coloured or cloudy), it's time to go to the spirit cut. Another manual check is rubbing some spirit between hands, then inhaling two or three times from cupped hands, which reveals different aromas each time.

'Bruichladdich new make spirit character has a sea spray note, ozone freshness, linen brought in from the washing line, and it's the same in Port Charlotte and Octomore but not more pronounced in peated spirit, so it's not coming from the peat,' says Adam Hannett. Other variants

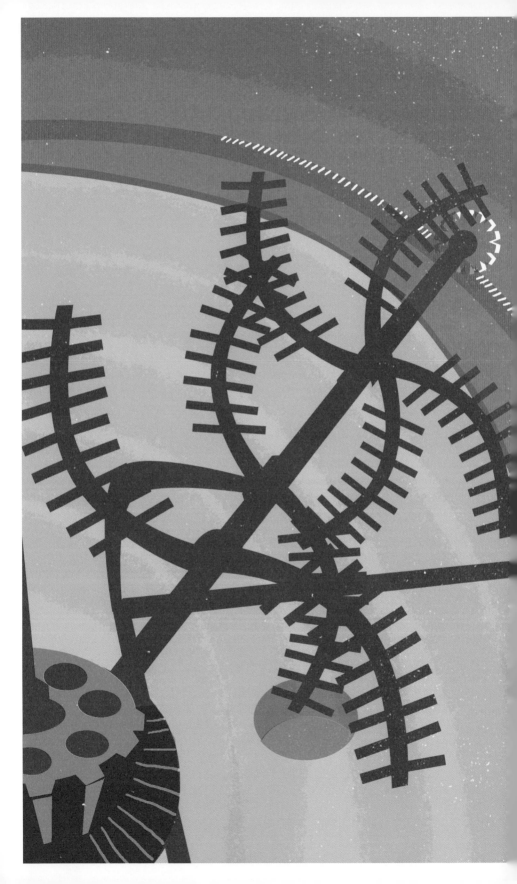

also have specific characteristics. 'You pick up differences in new make spirit depending on the origin of the barley. Single farms supply us from different regions – Aberdeen is more fruity with stewed pears, Lothian more biscuity, cereal, earthy, Black Isle more apples, croissant, brioche. Bere was porridge and Weetabix. This was part of the Single Farm Regional Trials Series.'

Another aspect is the mouthfeel. 'In the Bere barley, organic and biodynamic new make spirit, the viscosity is amplified a bit.'

Maturing malt whisky

When Bruichladdich reopened in 2001, around 70–75 per cent of the cask inventory was remade hogsheads, meaning bourbon barrels were upsized from a 200-litre (44-gallon) capacity to 250 litres (55 gallons). The focus now, however, is on first- and second-fill bourbon barrels, and first- and second-fill sherry casks. The oldest casks in the inventory date from 1964.

The Ternary Project is a small-batch bottling and distillery exclusive by name and by nature. Three components comprise three vintages of Bruichladdich, Port Charlotte and Octomore, with an amazing array of cask influences in the recipe. Bruichladdich accounts for 30 per cent of the recipe and includes bourbon barrel, French red wine casks and Pedro Ximénez sherry butts. Port Charlotte accounts for 40 per cent of the recipe aged in first-fill bourbon, first-fill Oloroso and first-fill virgin oak; Octomore 30 per cent, aged in Sauternes casks, Mourvèdre red wine barrels, Austrian sweet wine casks and Amarone and bourbon barrels. In brief, it delivers smoke, figs and toasted oak aromas. The palate has citrus and marine notes, and it has a sustained finish with smoke and dried fruit.

The 11 ageing warehouses have tin roofs, which allow the ambient temperature to have a greater impact on the interior, and promote a greater range of higher and lower temperatures; even during 24 hours the heat of the day can see the cask staves contracting slightly in the heat, then expanding in the cool of the night, in both racked and dunnage. And what about sea air coming into the ageing warehouses? Can this supplement the sea spray notes already evident in the new make spirit?

'Maritime air is drawn into the headspace within the cask, and some days more air gets in than others. You can lick your lips and taste the sea spray in the ageing warehouses. I believe the sea air does have an impact,' says Adam. But some new make spirit can have a head start in terms of maritime character. 'When I work with Islay barley, I find a maritime element due to the location the barley is grown in – there is an element of sea spray in the soil. And maturing on the island gives all the casks a maritime character,' he adds.

Bruichladdich tasting notes

Bruichladdich Classic Laddie 50% abv

Nose: Fresh and immediately malty, digestive biscuits and croissant, then wood smoke and wood embers, followed by crème brûlée, dry cider and a small bowl of muesli with raisins.

Palate: An overture of distinct but controlled sweetness continues with a luscious texture, releasing brioche, pain au chocolat and flapjacks, hints of aniseed and clove, culminating with poached fruits in syrup, while dry oak provides foundations.

Finish: Light sweetness, dryness, then richness, which melds into lusciousness with digestive biscuits and plums.

Bruichladdich Islay Barley 2013 50% abv

Nose: Lightly earthy overtones, damp forest that soon moves to an orchard, with apples, pears and pear drops making a stylish entrance; then digestive biscuits and muesli take centre stage, but are rapidly replaced by fresh apple juice and pears. These two notes form a cycle that repeats: digestive biscuits and muesli one moment, fresh apple juice and pears the next.

Palate: Ultra-smooth mouthfeel with a hint of vanilla custard, a medley of croissants, pain au chocolat and digestive biscuits open up, then pear drops come through with a wave of juicy, crisp green apples, lemon tart makes a brief appearance, then dry oak continues.

Finish: Rich dried fruit, apricots, prunes and orange marmalade, with toasted oak at the base.

Bruichladdich 15 year old 46% abv

Nose: Sherry trifle, sea salt, ripe banana, with creamy vanilla custard, then a floral interlude of lavender and violets, before oak and maltiness emerge.

Palate: Velvety mouthfeel yields sweet digestive biscuits, then zesty lemon teams up with sea salt; richness joins in with butterscotch and tropical fruits, with a hint of coconut.

Finish: Maltiness and smoke enhance each other, then keep going and going.

Bruichladdich 1986 Valinch 15 year old, cask strength 54.5% abv, Oloroso sherry cask

Nose: Vanilla, sherry, fresh tar, sticky toffee pudding, muscovado sugar and rich nutty fruit cake.

Palate: Like a rich, luscious dessert of butterscotch, fruit cake with a hint of sea salt, garnished with lemon, underpinned by toasty notes, juicy raisins, fruity, nutty, muscovado, gingerbread; really characterful.

Finish: Elegant, complex and sustained.

Bruichladdich Octomore 13.1 59.2% abv

Nose: Controlled, streamlined barbecue notes with English breakfast tea leaves, crème caramel opens up, joined by peaches and apricots, then all the flavours come into alignment, equally balanced, garnished by lightly earthy damp forest.

Palate: Elegant mouthfeel presents a broad panorama: barbecue notes and sea salt open up with juicy lusciousness, dried fruit and malty notes, well organized with small nuances of extra-virgin olive oil and anchovies popping up within the big picture, which remains constant.

Finish: Juicy, luscious richness balanced by barbecue notes that extend in a sweet-rich-dry-savoury balance.

Bruichladdich 1970, cask strength 45.8% abv

Nose: Coconut, pear drops and orange zest open the show, then amazing lemon appears, followed by creamy fruit trifle and rich set honey, vanilla pod and a hint of clove.

Palate: Ultra-delicate mouthfeel, with luscious vanilla, vibrant fresh lemon juice and ripe orange sweetness, then creamy fruit trifle and coconut, extending into dark chocolate. Evolves while retaining elegance.

Finish: Dynamic vanilla, dark chocolate and creamy trifle provide an animated, perky conclusion.

Chapter Nine

Caol Ila

Chapter Nine

Caol Ila

Visiting Caol Ila for the first time in 1997, I was mesmerized by a slender waterfall tumbling acrobatically down a long, sheer rock face. I assumed this was nature's contribution to the visuals, but it's also a water source for the distillery. What a way to arrive! When I returned to Caol Ila in 2006 during Fèis Ìle and again in 2023, I stood on the same spot each time to marvel at the cascading water. I had been and gone, but the waterfall was constant, and flowing water is a poignant metaphor for time passing. Remembering my previous visits, I thought of changes that had taken place at the distillery, on Islay and in my appreciation of whisky. I learned how to pronounce *Cull-Eela* on my first visit, but however many times I might visit a distillery there is always more to learn and more questions to ask. And the best people to learn from are all in the distillery.

Origins and expressions

Hector Henderson was a Glasgow entrepreneur who was a partner in Littlemill, a distillery in the Lowlands, but he resigned from this in order to finance a distillery at Caol Ila. The site needed funding, as it was cut out of the rock face, which then provided stone for the buildings when it was founded in 1846. The distillery was built on the site of established shipping routes to and from Islay and Glasgow, which provided a significant trading advantage. But bankruptcy followed, and Hector sold the distillery in 1852 to Norman Buchanan. And in 1863, when Buchanan found himself bankrupt, he sold Caol Ila to Bulloch Lade & Co., a wine and spirit merchant in Glasgow that created blends for private customers, able to draw on extensive stocks, including 10 and 15 year old whiskies, which were then considered unusually senior.

In 1859, Bulloch Lade & Co. bought another distillery, Camlachie near Glasgow, and the vendor happened to be the original owner of Caol Ila – Hector Henderson. The company then built Benmore distillery in Campbeltown, operational in 1868, before focussing on Caol Ila in 1879. An extensive refurbishment included a malt barn that was 36 metres (39 yards) long, 24 metres (26 yards) wide and four storeys high. The top two floors stored malted barley and the other two storeys were the malting floors, with two kilns installed. A state-of- the-art pier was also built, which enabled puffers to dock and load, even in 3-metre (10-feet) tides.

In the 1880s, Caol Ila was producing 147,000 gallons annually. But even this amount could not satisfy demand from Scotland and England, and it was put on allocation. In 1920, Bulloch Lade & Co. went into voluntary liquidation and the distillery was acquired by Caol Ila Distillery Co., a consortium that was managed by Robertson & Baxter, which also owned Bunnahabhain (see pages 121-2). In 1927, the Distillers Company Ltd (an amalgamation of Scotch whisky distilleries) took ownership of Caol Ila.

The Great Depression of the early 1930s led to the distillery being silent from 1930, but it was restarted in 1934. That was when a regular visitor, the *Pibroch*, first arrived. This was a puffer running a dedicated service for Caol Ila, transporting coal, barley and empty casks to the distillery, then returning to Glasgow with filled casks.

Everything changed in 1972 when the entire distillery was demolished, including the floor maltings. The *Pibroch* left the pier for the final time. Only the ageing warehouses remained. The distillery was rebuilt in a spirit of great optimism that sales of blended Scotch were booming, and greater quantities of malt whisky were needed. Caol Ila was the last distillery in the Distillers Company to be modernized. Rebuilding took two years, with new stills an exact copy of the original wash and spirit still, plus the addition of three more pairs of wash and spirit stills.

When it reopened in 1974, Caol Ila had 32 employees including an exciseman, and was producing seven days a week. Malted barley no longer arrived at the pier, and casks no longer departed from there either. Port Ellen Maltings supplied barley, and casks were driven to the main ferry terminal. However, a downturn in Scotch whisky sales in the 1980s reduced the working week to four days.

Caol Ila enjoyed a moment in the spotlight when a programme of limited editions called Rare Malts launched in 1996 and featured a Caol Ila 20 year old distilled in 1975, and the following two years saw a Caol Ila 21 year old distilled in 1975, then a Caol Ila 20 year old distilled in 1977.

In 2002, Caol Ila was one of four Hidden Malts released by the Distillers Company. Together with one expression each from Glen Ord, Glen Elgin and Clynelish, the Hidden Malts release included three expressions of Caol Ila: a 12 year old, an 18 year old and a cask-strength expression. These limited editions led to three continually available expressions of Caol Ila launching in 2002, comprising a 12 year old with gentle sea breeze and smoke emerging, an 18 year old offering balanced smoke and a cask strength yielding medicinal and sea salt notes. At Fèis Ìle in 2006, a Caol Ila distilled in 1993 was launched, which had spent several months in a Moscatel cask that added rich fruit to the sweetness and smoke.

Caol Ila's long history meant that generations of the same families have worked there, and one bottling paid tribute to a particular person and his family. The Caol Ila Stitchell Reserve Unpeated, one of the 2013 special releases, marked Billy Stitchell's 40-year service at Caol Ila. Born on Islay, Billy joined Caol Ila in 1974. Was this his destiny? Billy's father and paternal grandfather had worked at Caol Ila, and his maternal grandfather and great-grandfather had both been head malt man there.

The current distillery manager, Samuel Hale, was appointed in 2020. Samuel was already on Islay, having worked at Port Ellen Maltings since

2018, initially as trainee site operations manager, then as maltings manager. His career in Scotch whisky dates from 2017, when he began at Burghead Maltings in 2017 in the Elgin area of Speyside.

'I have a love for the malting process, as it's so hands-on, and I was very happy at Port Ellen Maltings. But if there is an opportunity, I believe in jumping in. That's why I applied for the job at Caol Ila, and I love it here, the team, the location. I always wanted to work on an island such as Islay; I like quiet living and love the outdoors,' Samuel says.

The role of a distillery manager also entails the opposite of quiet living! Personal appearances to present and host tastings at whisky festivals and special events throughout the year and around the world are expected. 'I love getting to know people and getting a conversation going. It's about sharing experiences,' he further explains.

On 25 August 2022, the new visitor experience, including a cafe converted from a former warehouse, officially opened. As an incorrigible observer, I could sit with a coffee and monitor proceedings in this spacious, stylish space. The cafe serves great coffee, full-bodied and full of flavour, which matters as I am also a coffee lover (flavours in general fascinate me, whether to drink or eat).

One important visitor at Caol Ila, who arrived in 2022 and staying permanently, is a Johnnie Walker striding man sculpture. His apparel is classic Savile Row tailoring, but with Islay styling. The frock coat has been painted with a seascape, while the boots have been 'peated', in the sense of being decorated with an Islay landscape and peat bank. This was the work of an Islay artist, Rosemary Fletcher, together with her daughters, Cairistiona Rose and Jessica May. The relationship between Johnnie Walker and Caol Ila is close and longstanding, with the earliest reference to Caol Ila in the John Walker & Sons inventory dating from 1897. And there's no lack of commitment. Up to 90 per cent of Caol Ila's annual production adds something special to the Johnnie Walker recipe.

'Caol Ila has always been a massive part of Johnnie Walker, but its role depends on the expression,' says Emma Walker, Johnnie Walker's master blender. 'Johnnie Walker Red Label explores the distillery character, and is more about exuberance, with freshness and smoke complementing spice. In Blue Label the smoke is tempered but still powerful, and this extends the sense of richness.'

Caol Ila is also one of the 'four corners of Scotland', which represent regional malt whisky styles, together with Glenkinchie for the Lowlands, Cardhu for Speyside and Clynelish for the Highlands. These malts also provide an insight into the Johnnie Walker recipe, to which they all contribute in their characteristic way.

Crafting spirit

Caol Ila distills up to 6.5 million litres (1.4 million gallons) of alcohol annually, which is more than any other distillery on Islay, though there is no sense of being in a 'high-volume production unit'. In fact, the distillery has an air of tranquillity, enhanced by views along the Sound of Islay.

Malt is supplied by Port Ellen Maltings, which is Laureate peated to 38–40 ppm using peat from Glenegedale. A Porteus mill dating from 1962 produces a standard milling specification of 20 per cent husk, 70 per cent grits and 10 per cent fines, dispatched to a stainless steel mash tun.

Distilleries usually use either wooden or stainless steel washbacks; having both on the premises is unusual. But that's the case at Caol Ila. Eight Oregon pine washbacks each have a 53,000-litre (11,700-gallon) capacity, alongside two stainless steel washbacks with a 51,000-litre (11,200-gallon) capacity. Current production is seven days a week, with a 60-hour fermentation time. 'There's no real difference between the wash using Oregon pine and stainless steel with the fermentation profiles being the same for both vessels,' observes Samuel.

The stills are pear-shaped with tall, wide necks, creating plenty of reflux and additional fruit flavours. The lyne arm offers a different influence: a slight descent encourages a broader range of flavour compounds to continue to the condensers, which are shell and tube.

In comparison to the size of the stills, the fill volume is low. The consequence is a larger area of copper available to interact with the vapours, promoting a fruitier spirit.

Maturing malt whisky

The new make spirit aroma is distinctly smoky, with ripe fruit, a hint of sea spray and brine. The palate has an elegant sweetness, with smoky, ripe fruit and lemony, sea spray tang. New make spirit isn't filled into casks at Caol Ila; rather, it's filled into tankers at the distillation strength and transported to ageing warehouses on the mainland. On arrival the new make spirit is reduced to 63.5% abv for ageing, usually in second-fill Bourbon barrels, and aged in warehouses on the mainland. A small number of casks are aged at Caol Ila, currently between 100 and 200, most of which were filled in 2012.

A batch of unpeated spirit was also produced from 1997-2005, for 8–12 weeks each year. Production was the same as for peated malt, including the spirit cut. However, some preparation was also required. Rinsing and flushing the existing phenolics out of the pipework and the system took approximately three weeks of production. It then took about two weeks of peated production to rebuild the usual level of phenolics in the system.

The profile of unpeated spirit included creamy, malty and grass notes. This is not the equivalent of peated spirit minus the phenolics, as the balance and visibility of flavours differed.

Which age of Caol Ila is best depends entirely on personal preference, as the smoke reduces with ageing. This was demonstrated by a tasting I attended at the distillery, comparing different ages matured in bourbon barrels.

A 4 year old revealed more of the distillery character, before the cask influence had gained momentum. On the nose, smoke overlays fruit, particularly baked apples and a hint of pear drops, while the palate shows smoke and fruit with a distinct salty lemon tang.

A 12 year old released a medley of aromas, smoke and brine, with hints of pear drops, baked apples and liquorice. The palate delivered smokiness, baked apples, vanilla, pear drops and a hint of honey. An 18 year old revealed the same characteristics but with the addition of fudge, digestive biscuits and lemon zest.

Caol Ila tasting notes

Caol Ila Moch 43% abv

Nose: Sweet and savoury combination, with toffee apples, popcorn and roasted nuts, then juicy green olives in brine; an initial hint of vanilla that soon grows, accompanied by lemon meringue and garnished by lemon zest.

Palate: Ultra-mellow mouthfeel, sweet-rich-dry balance that features lemon tart, poached dried fruit in syrup, then an individual apricot note, followed by orange marmalade, a hint of green olives in brine garnished with zesty lemon, underlying toast and dry oak.

Finish: Very mellow olives, extra-virgin olive oil and walnuts, then dryness and toastiness join in.

Caol Ila 12 year old 43% abv

Nose: Vanilla rises above a platform of oak and toast, then a bouquet of roses followed by digestive biscuits, a burst of limes and grapefruit.

Palate: Soft mouthfeel becomes lightly creamy, elegant apricots nestle in vanilla; really juicy, sweet oranges turning into orange marmalade, suffused with gentle smoke and dryness adding structure.

Finish: Fresh, tangy, citrus juiciness, with toasted oak and a gentle waft of barbecue notes.

Caol Ila 14 year old unpeated 59.3% abv

One of the special releases in 2012, this was the first Caol Ila released as a 14 year old, and the first aged in first-fill ex-bodega European oak sherry casks.

Nose: Gingerbread, maltiness and oak with a hint of raisin and toasted oak.

Palate: Delicate, luxurious caramel, toasted oak, raisins and luscious dried fruit, then a little dark chocolate, a hint of nuttiness and more raisins, more dried fruit and fruit cake.

Finish: A burst of dryness and maltiness, then oak and mellow spice.

Caol Ila 18 year old unpeated 59.8% abv

Nose: Toasted, roasted nuts are a solo act, then a chorus line of chocolate brownie, rich chocolate truffles and rum and raisin ice cream joins in, then moves to linseed oil with a gentle waft of smoke.

Palate: Fresh, soft mouthfeel; amazing sweetness opens up on a puff of smoke, releasing chocolate truffles, raisins, prunes and sticky toffee pudding. A rich and intense medley wrapped in soft smoke.

Finish: Light and tangy, with raisins and prunes, then dry-roasted nuts come through with sweetness and richness.

Chapter Ten

ili

Chapter Ten

ili

All distilleries share many characteristics, and every distillery also has its own individuality, but few have a superlative to quote. ili has one. This will be Islay's smallest distillery, producing 200,000 litres (44,000 gallons) of pure alcohol per annum. The distillery will be powered by renewable energy generated on site, and will be the first in Scotland to offer a community benefit fund. Projected to be operational by 2026, the new make spirit will span various peating levels.

Planning permission was granted in December 2022 for a circular stone and timber building with overtones of Stonehenge splendour. Roughly textured stone repurposed from redundant farm buildings will be used to build the walls, with an extensive full-height glass frontage providing a focal point from the exterior, while providing views of Loch Gearach from the interior.

Designed by Alan Higgs Architects in London, the ground floor will include a cafe, shop and tasting area at the centre of the building. The lower ground floor will house production and offices, while a separate dunnage warehouse will be a timber construction.

A circular distillery building is unusual on Islay – and in Scotland – square and rectangular being the norm, although Islay has prime examples of circular buildings. These include Bowmore's Kilarrow

Church (known as 'the round church'), which has been open for worship since 1769, and is thought to have been inspired by churches in Tuscany. There are two lighthouses: Ruvaal on the north-eastern tip of Islay, dating from 1859, and Rinns of Islay on the tiny island of Orsay, a few hundred metres from the southern coast of Islay; this was completed in 1825 by the distinguished civil engineer Robert Stevenson, who designed numerous lighthouses in Scotland.

The distillery site occupies 2 hectares (5 acres) of Gearach Farm near Port Charlotte, acquired in 2008 by Bertram Nesselrode. He had enjoyed annual holidays on Islay since 2003 and attended Fèis Ìle a number of times. 'When I started visiting Islay I drank Bruichladdich, initially Port Charlotte, and I met Mark Reynier (then Bruichladdich's CEO). You fall in love with one distillery, and then explore them all. I also drank Bunnahabhain, which was popular with keepers and farmers I met on Islay and working on the west coast, and I think Ardbeg is fantastic. The more you understand why something tastes as it does, the more interesting it is,' says Bertram.

Visits to Islay changed from personal to professional in 2018, after Bertram decided to open a distillery in partnership with his neighbour, Scott McLellan, an Ileach who farms next door at Kilchiaran with his father, Neil. Neither has a malt whisky background, but Bertram, originally from Germany, is a plant biology graduate of Edinburgh University. Scott has an interest in industrial processes, having worked offshore as a night drilling supervisor after graduating from the University of Strathclyde with an MEng in Aero-Mechanical Engineering.

'The fundamentals of making whisky are a biological and chemical process, which fascinated me as an undergraduate, and I started home brewing in 2018, which equates to the first part of the whisky-making process. Yeast together with cask selection provide a range of things to explore,' Bertram says.

Barley will be sourced locally (as much as possible), with fields at Gearach farm already drained, using the original Victorian system of clay pipes, to prepare the ground for sowing barley. At Kilchiaran, Neil and Scott already grow barley for Islay's distilleries. Gearach Farm also provides grazing for Scott and Neil's prizewinning herds of Blackface sheep and Limousin–Highland crossbreed cattle. The equipment commissioned includes a mill able to process 500 kg (1,100 lb) per hour, a mash tun with a 0.5-tonne capacity, six washbacks (whether wooden or stainless steel remains to be seen), each with a 5,000-litre (1,100-gallon) capacity, and a wash still and spirit still with a 2,500-litre (550-gallon) and 1,800-litre (400-gallon) capacity respectively.

The name of the distillery, ili, is the oldest recorded name for Islay and was inspired by Norse remains recently discovered at Olestad, a prehistoric settlement with a Viking name on Bertram's farm. Olestad is being excavated by archaeologists led by Professor Steven Mithen from Reading University, who also began a three-year excavation of the distillery site in 2022. Let's hope for some exciting discoveries.

Chapter Eleven

Kilchoman

Chapter Eleven

Kilchoman

Origins and expressions

History is an integral element of a distillery's identity – although history is relative. What makes it interesting are the events that take place and the people involved, whether the history begins in 1805 or in 2005, when Kilchoman opened.

Kilchoman already has a rich heritage, and the present is history in the making. The protagonist who established Kilchoman, the first newly built distillery on Islay for 124 years, is Anthony Wills. An Englishman, he spent 15 years in the wine trade before moving from England to Scotland in 1995. He also moved from wine to whisky, becoming an independent bottler releasing single-cask single malts, such as Bowmore and Caol Ila, under the label Caledonian Selection. Sales took off, but by the start of the millennium sourcing casks had become increasingly difficult. It was a turning point.

'I decided to build my own distillery, and didn't dig too deep into the challenges, even though my accountant warned me off and people thought I was mad,' Anthony says. 'But I had a clear vision, and location was very important in that. Islay had a reputation around the world, so I knew people would at least look at my whisky just because it was from Islay.'

Bruichladdich was the only other Islay distillery that was independent then; all the others were owned by multinationals. Anthony saw independence as an advantage, but it comes at a price. Or rather, independence means raising the necessary funds to ensure it.

'Investors wanted a three- to five-year turnaround, not a 15-year investment, and there were times when we didn't think we'd get there. I took a risk and decided that rather than waiting for all the funding in order to start, I would have to start in order to get the rest of the funding.' And that entailed paying a price personally. 'The early days were very stressful. It was three years of juggling. One advantage of a new distillery is having a blank piece of paper, but there was also no template for a new distillery and a lot of unknowns. Now when people come to ask me for advice I say: raise twice the amount of money you need, don't cut corners and don't try and do it on a shoestring.'

The concept was to establish a new distillery that took production back to its roots, when a distillery worked in tandem with a farm. 'You can compete with more established distilleries in your own way if you're doing something different. We're producing a single malt from barley grown on a single farm, in fields surrounding the distillery, and undertaking every stage of the whisky-making process at the distillery, including traditional floor malting. Kilchoman is the only distillery in Scotland doing this,' states Anthony.

Planning permission was granted in 2002, building work began in 2004 and the distillery was operational in November 2005. The late Dr Jim Swann, a whisky consultant par excellence with a global following, designed the equipment in order to produce a classic Islay style: smoky and peaty, but also fruity. Anthony explains: 'It was emotional when the first new make spirit flowed on 29 November 2005, and the first cask was filled on 14 December. We still have Cask No. 1, which is a refill bourbon barrel from Speyside cooperage. By the end of 2005 we'd filled seven casks with new make spirit. Production then grew to 50,000 litres in 2006. In 2022 it was 600,000 litres.'

Barley was floor-malted at the distillery and also supplied by Port Ellen Maltings. 'Our production regime is the same whether we are distilling malt from Port Ellen or our own farm barley, but they are very different. Islay barley has a fresh malty flavour; Port Ellen malt is richer in character.'

Kilchoman made its debut in September 2009, with the release of a 3 year old malt aged initially in bourbon barrels and the final six months in sherry casks. In 2011, the inaugural 100 per cent Islay malt was launched, distilled from barley cultivated in the surrounding fields, aged in first-fill and refill bourbon barrels. Two new ongoing expressions of Kilchoman were subsequently released: the first was Machir Bar in 2012, a peated malt aged in bourbon and sherry casks. The second, in 2013, was Loch Gorm, aged entirely in sherry casks. That year also saw the release of what was then Kilchoman's oldest whisky, a 6 year old, with hints of butterscotch and soft citrus fruit, followed by a peaty, fruity finish. This was the 2007 vintage, of which 10,000 bottles were available.

Kilchoman became very much a family enterprise in 2015, when Anthony and wife Kathy (who works in the accounts department) welcomed their eldest son, George, to the company to develop UK sales. Their other two sons, James and Peter, were already on board for sales and marketing. That year also saw another family link celebrated, with the release of the Land Rover bottling. Kathy's grandfather, Spencer Wilks, owned Laggan Estate a few miles from the town of Bowmore, and was also managing director of the Rover car company from 1928–67. His younger brother, Maurice, was an engineer, and together they designed a vehicle that could negotiate Islay's terrain and roads. A name for this vehicle was provided by the Laggan Estate's head gamekeeper, Ian Fraser, who spontaneously referred to it as a 'land rover'. Production of the Land Rover model began in 1948, and a Royal Warrant from King George VI followed in 1951.

In 2014, a specially designed Land Rover conveyed George Wills around the UK to conduct tastings of Kilchoman. A limited edition of

468 bottles marked this: Machir Bay Land Rover Tour 2014, a single-cask, cask strength at 58.5% abv. The tour was such a success that the following year it was repeated and accompanied by another single-cask bottling, Machir Bay Land Rover Tour 2015, at a cask strength of 58.8% abv, a limited edition of 648 bottles.

Production capacity increased significantly at the distillery in 2017, when a four-month build resulted in a new malting floor and kiln. This has double the capacity of the previous malting floor, enabling up to 4 tonnes to be malted per week, and so twice the amount of new make spirit. In 2019, there was another doubling when a new building was constructed alongside the existing stillhouse, which formed a second stillhouse, accommodating two new stills that duplicated the size and shape of the existing two stills. This also provides more scope for innovation.

'It's important to keep offering expressions that differ from the continually available range,' Anthony says, 'and we release four limited editions annually, plus a special bottling for Kilchoman's Club members.'

Crafting spirit

Despite being the first new distillery to be built on Islay for 124 years, the concept is entirely traditional, combining a distillery with a farm that supplies barley. 'I'd been coming to Islay for years, and the land here is perfect for growing the barley I wanted,' observes Anthony. 'It's wet and windy, but the sandy soil drains well, and farm distilleries did it in the old days. In a bad year you get less barley; the quantity is affected, but not the quality.'

Rockside Farm comprises 930 hectares (2,300 acres), surrounding the ruins of Kilchoman church, of which the most fertile land is 162 hectares (400 acres) surrounding the distillery. Rockside Farm has supplied barley to Kilchoman since 2005 and was purchased by Anthony in 2015. Various barley varieties have been cultivated, including Optic, Golden Promise, Publican, Concerto and Laureate. Concerto and Publican were always very consistent, with Sassy replacing Concerto in 2022. The timetable means that the harvest gathered in 2021 was malted from January 2022 and distilled from November.

When I visited Kilchoman at the end of 2022, I picked up what I thought was a small booklet. It unfolded into the size of an A3 (tabloid size) page with a map of the farmland, indicating the name and size of each individual field, which barley variety was cultivated there in 2022, the expected harvest and how many barrels this could fill once distilled. High Machrie Field, for example, is 5.7 hectares (14 acres), sown with Sassy, with an expected harvest of 32 tonnes that could fill 84 barrels. I was thrilled to have this; it's a wonderful advance in the level of detail that is being provided. And all of us whisky fans love it.

The barley is transported in chariots (which resemble deep wheelbarrows with very large wheels) and is initially amassed in the centre of the concrete malting floor, creating a bed 60 cm (2 ft) deep. There it remains for 10–12 hours to allow the natural heat of germination to accumulate. The malt is then spread evenly across the entire malting floor, creating a bed about 10–15 cm (4–6 in) deep. A rake is pulled through the bed to aerate it and prevent overheating; another form of aeration and temperature control during the summer is opening windows.

Kindling is used to start a fire in the kiln, to which peat, including caff, is added. Peat is hand-cut from a peat bank by the shores of Loch Gorm between April and July by Derek Scott, one of Kilchoman's maltsters. The kiln has double doors that can be opened to allow air in and intensify the fire, while a fan above the perforated floor of the kiln helps draw smoke through the bed.

The Porteus mill began its career in a Yorkshire brewery, then relocated to Kilchoman, which means that the grist it now produces leads to malt whisky rather than beer (perhaps this was always the dream of this particular mill). Grist is produced to the usual specification of 70 per cent grits, 20 per cent husk and 10 per cent fines. A total of 14 stainless steel washbacks each have a 6,000-litre (1,300-gallon) capacity, with stainless steel chosen for ease of cleaning.

'We experimented with fresh yeast, which gives a creamier result, while pressed yeast gives more fruity, floral notes. Mauri [distiller's yeast] generates a huge amount of apples and honeycomb in the wash,' says Anthony. Fermentation lasts an average of 85 hours and produces a wash at 8% abv.

'New make spirit is creamy, citrus, clean with maritime character that comes through more after a few years of ageing,' Anthony explains. 'We distill malt from our own malting floors separately from malt supplied by Port Ellen Maltings, and although the spirit is similar from both, Kilchoman malt produces spirit with greater freshness, but is not as creamy as Port Ellen. New make spirit from Port Ellen and Kilchoman malt is collected in dedicated receivers so that there is no crossover between the two.'

The pot ale and spent lees remaining after each distillation are allowed to be spread on the fields as a fertilizer, but only limited quantities are permitted.

Maturing malt whisky

Casks are filled by hand, with bourbon barrels sourced from Breckenridge distillery in Colorado, and sherry casks from José y Miguel Martín, the renowned bodega in Jerez, Spain. Comparing the influence of these two cask types, first-fill bourbon gives more citrus and lemon alongside the phenolics. First-fill sherry casks promote smoky, peaty characteristics with spicy richness from Oloroso casks, and distinct nuttiness from Fino casks. Using first-fill bourbon and sherry casks also means a growing number of casks available to refill and gain different influences.

Cognac casks are also used for full maturation, which is rare among malts, as well as STR casks, which stands for Shave, Toast, Rechar. This means shaving the interior surface of a wine barrique (typically red wine) to reveal a fresh surface. Toasting and recharring the surface entails intense heat that caramelizes residual wine within the staves, and this adds intense red fruit to a malt within a few years of ageing. STR casks are a relatively recent innovation, pioneered by Dr Swann, and supplied by J. Dias cooperage in Portugal to a growing number of malt whisky distilleries.

Five dunnage warehouses with ventilation grates at floor level have casks stacked three high, which means each tier experiences the same conditions. There are also two racked warehouses with air flow promoted by ventilation grates at floor level and in the roof. Casks are stacked six high in one and nine high in another, which means relatively cooler, more humid conditions on the ground floor. The results are classic Islay.

'Maritime and peated character are intertwined. A lot of salty, briny, barbecue on the beach notes come from the character of the peat, and our peat has the greatest influence on the resulting whisky. But we mature everything on site, and there is a lot of salt in the air, even though we're the only distillery not actually on the coast, and sea air is bound to have an effect over time.'

How Kilchoman shows after longer ageing remains to be seen. I very much look forward to sampling a 21 and a 25 year old, which are only a few years away. 'The cask influence builds up over time, while the peaty character drops off; older is not always better, it's different,' Anthony remarks. 'If you want maritime vibrancy, it's best to drink Kilchoman relatively younger, 7–12 years is perfect. Any older than this and the maritime character is mellower.'

Kilchoman tasting notes

Machir Bay 46% abv

Nose: Fresh and rich, combining fruity and malty notes, extending with linseed and Brazil nuts, evolving into fruit and nut chocolate, cappuccino notes and a hint of smoke, sea breeze and brine.

Palate: Rich, dried fruit arrives reclining on an elegant mouthfeel, then a medley begins: lemon tart, dark chocolate, with a luscious layer of sweetness above, and a platform of dryness beneath. Wafting, underlying smoke and olive brine add range.

Finish: Fresh, light sweetness, richness, then dryness and muesli step in.

Sanaig 46% abv

Nose: Elegant combination of creamy fruit trifle and tiramisu, merging into nougat, biscotti, espresso and dark chocolate, then evolving effortlessly into savoury olive notes and a background waft of smoke. Remains elegant but concentrated.

Palate: Very elegant and delicate mouthfeel, releasing sweetness and richness; smoky barbecue notes, with a savoury core spanning olives and grilled peppers, with a hint of anchovies; underlying dryness is restrained, but adds balance and structure.

Finish: Gentle dryness leads, then sweet-savoury notes continue, with savoury moving to the forefront and sweetness receding.

Loch Gorm 46% abv

Nose: Fresh, ripe fruit and caramelized fruit, toffee apples and distinct biscuit notes that move into Ovaltine and digestive biscuits, with smoke and tar adding range and balance.

Palate: Fruitiness with a very soft mouthfeel; smoke gently wafts into the forefront, underlined by toasted and chargrilled notes and balanced by panna cotta creaminess; flapjacks and muesli before fruit makes an entrance in the form of apricots and orange marmalade, with oak dryness throughout.

Finish: Fruity richness with flapjack, muesli, dried fruits in syrup and chargrilled notes that begin quietly, then become louder.

Kilchoman 100% Islay 12th Edition Single Farm 50% abv

Nose: Prunes and maltiness establish richness and freshness; cottage loaf interplays with cereal and oak notes and a hint of muesli, with embers and chargrilled notes throughout.

Palate: Ultra-soft mouthfeel, delicate flavours move gradually into the foreground and announce themselves: apricot Danish pastry, lemon tart and apple pie enhanced by underlying dryness, with chargrilled lightly earthy notes driving the palate forward.

Finish: Opens with a fruit cake note accompanied by balancing dryness, a sip of cappuccino and chargrilled notes.

Chapter Twelve

Lagavulin

Chapter Twelve

Lagavulin

Otters and seals play in Lagavulin Bay, where two promontories reach out like eager arms trying to embrace the sea. Two monuments face each other across the bay. One is Dunyvaig Castle, now a romantic ruin, though the courtyard and the keep are still discernible. Originating in the twelfth century, the castle served as the stronghold of the Macdonalds, who were Lords of the Isles (a kingdom that included Islay, Skye, Arran and Bute). A fleet of galleys moored in the bay patrolled this kingdom. In 1677, the Campbells of Cawdor, who owned the castle, dismantled it, having built Islay House – a stately home near Bridgend – as their seat. Facing the remains of the castle is a monument to the past, present and the future of malt whisky: Lagavulin distillery.

Origins and expressions

Lagavulin was founded by John Johnston, an Islay farmer and initially an illicit distiller who managed to evade excisemen on numerous occasions by hiding his stills and casks in a church. The church bells were rung as a warning to those who needed to be warned that the exciseman was nearing the island. However, Johnston had aroused suspicion, and tougher penalties for illicit distilling were introduced in 1816. That was the year he was caught in the act, and the exciseman gave him an ultimatum: get a distilling licence, or get a prison sentence. Lagavulin was licensed in 1816.

Johnston took on a partner in 1835, James L Mackie, and the following year Johnston died. Lagavulin was acquired by Alexander Graham, a spirits merchant from Glasgow who also owned pubs in the city. He paid £1,103, 9 shillings and 8 pence. In 1861, the lease for the distillery and farm passed to James L Mackie in partnership with Captain Graham, a relative of Alexander Graham. An addition to the team was Mackie's nephew, Peter, son of a distiller, who worked at Lagavulin from 1878. Renowned for his hard work and commitment to quality, he was known as 'restless Pete'.

He took over the distillery in 1890, having created his own company, Mackie & Co., in the 1880s to market Lagavulin and blends he had created. Seeing the global potential for a Scotch whisky brand, he also launched a new blend in 1890, White Horse, in which Lagavulin was an important ingredient. The name was inspired by The White Horse Inn, a bohemian hub in Canongate, the street where Mackie's family owned a residence.

Another aspect of Peter's empire was purchasing large quantities of Laphroaig, based on an agreement in place for decades. But when Ian Hunter arrived at Laphroaig in 1907, he terminated the agreement. Demand for Laphroaig was growing, and developing its profile as a single malt, rather than being an 'invisible' component of a blend, was a more lucrative option. Peter sued. He lost. Then he decided to open a distillery to produce a heavily peated malt whisky exactly like Laphroaig. A vacant malt mill on the Lagavulin site provided the venue, and also a name: Malt Mill. The distillery shared Lagavulin's mash tun, but had its own dedicated pot stills, which replicated the size and shape of Laphroaig's, and he also hired Laphroaig's head brewer to distil malt whisky that was the same as Laphroaig. But it didn't achieve the same profile.

I've been wondering about Peter's motivation. There are no known bottlings of Malt Mill as a single malt; there is only a bottle of new make spirit on display at Lagavulin. Malt Mill was certainly used in blended Scotch, but documentation to confirm which blend(s) is lacking. It may have been a component of Ancient Scotch, another successful blend created by Mackie.

This suggests Peter didn't invest in Malt Mill to try and outsell Laphroaig. If he did this in order to be self-sufficient, and supply his own blends with a malt whisky similar to Laphroaig, it was a shrewd business decision. Did he also want to show Laphroaig that he didn't need them? Who knows.

Peter Mackie was made a baronet in 1920 and died in 1924. His eponymous company, Mackie & Co., became White Horse Distillers, and in 1927 part of Distillers Company Ltd, an amalgamation of Scottish whisky distilleries. This almost brought the Peter Mackie era to an end, except that Malt Mill remained operational.

Rebuilding work at Lagavulin began in 1951, but the following year an explosion and fire meant more rebuilding, and it wasn't until 1953 that it was back in production. Malt Mill was closed in 1962, and Lagavulin experienced a series of changes, with direct firing of the stills replaced by steam heating in 1969, and the floor maltings decommissioned in 1974. The downturn in sales of blended Scotch in the 1980s saw production decrease to four days a week, meaning six mashes.

A new era began at the end of that decade, with the launch of the Classic Malts in 1989. Lagavulin was one of six 'classic malts', along with Cragganmore, Dalwhinnie, Glenkinchie, Oban and Talisker, which together demonstrated the range of styles and flavours that malt whisky offered. The Special Releases programme of cask-strength, limited-edition malts released by Diageo in 2002 included two from Lagavulin: a 12 year old at 58% abv and a 25 year old at 57.2% abv, both bottled in 2002. This annual release was a showcase for Lagavulin, with a 12 year old in 2003, 2004 and again in 2005, and a 12 and 30 year old in 2006. And so it continued, with Lagavulin making regular appearances among the special releases.

The first Lagavulin distillery manager I met was Donald Renwick (1998–2005). He was very unassuming with a gentle manner, but always ready to discuss details, in detail, which I really appreciated.

I immediately liked Lagavulin the first time I visited. A stream that tumbles alongside the buildings appealed to my romantic side. But I am also practical, and so is the stream, as it conveys the distillery's water supply. The source is Lochan Sholum, just over two miles away, and this stream is the final leg of that journey.

In addition to visiting distilleries I enjoy visiting historic houses, and Lagavulin combines the two, having a 'guest wing' with a sense of a country house. One room could be a gentleman's or lady's study, a place to sit, read, reflect and sip malt whisky.

The 200th anniversary of the distillery in 2016 was marked by a special bottling. I was lucky enough to receive a small bottle of this, but I haven't tasted it yet. I'm a whisky lover and a collector. I want to taste it. But I also want to keep it in perfect, unopened condition in my collection. It's a difficult way to live.

A fascinating Islay–Mexican collaboration was launched in 2021. Lagavulin Jazz 2021 was the first Lagavulin finished in ex-mezcal casks. Mezcal is distilled from agave that has been cooked in open fires, giving it a smokiness. On the nose, unusual smoky-meaty aromas lead familiar Lagavulin linseed oil and fragrant smoke.

In April 2022, Jordan Paisley was appointed as distillery manager, just before Fèis Ìle. The annual festival bottling that year was a 12 year old, rich and full-bodied with maritime notes of crystalline salt and seaweed. 'I really enjoy hosting our tastings as the distillery manager, meeting our fans from around the world and enjoying a dram with them. My first Fèis Ìle was shortly after I joined the team, so it was a great opportunity to hear from Lagavulin fans first-hand about what makes this whisky so special,' Jordan says. He was born on Islay and attended Islay High School, then qualified as an engineer and travelled the world in the merchant navy. He returned to Islay in 2019.

'My first job in the industry was in November 2019, working for Diageo across projects at Lagavulin and Caol Ila distilleries and the Port Ellen Maltings. I started as the distillery manager at Lagavulin in March 2022. I'm originally from Islay and these iconic distilleries are part of local life. When the opportunity to be Lagavulin's manager came up, I had to go for it – it's a dream role.'

Lagavulin's past was evoked in an auction in 2022. A 5 cl bottle of Malt Mill 10 year old no. 2 malt whisky sold for £6,670 at Whisky.Auction. Malt Mill was in production from 1908–62, but it wasn't bottled as a single malt, instead being used as a component whisky in blended Scotch. This immediately gave it rarity appeal, and miniatures are likely to have been given as samples or gifts to customers rather than available to the public, which further enhances the rarity.

A miniature can be proportionately more expensive than a full-sized bottle, or even exceed the full-sized value. It will be a wonderful snapshot of a whisky from a particular era, should it ever be opened and sampled, but many such examples will not be opened.

Criticism of collectors is often based on the view that malt whisky is distilled to be enjoyed – but enjoying doesn't have to mean consuming. There's more than one way to enjoy a whisky, and possessing a bottle can be very rewarding. Particularly as a rare bottle has the additional status of an *objet d'art* and a historic monument, being monumental in terms of status if not size. Confirming authenticity of such a rare bottle involves provenance: examining the paper on which the label is printed, the ink, typeface and so on, and exploring as many archival sources as possible to corroborate.

Crafting spirit

Production capacity is 3.25 million litres (714,900 gallons) of new make spirit annually, which means 24.5 tonnes of malted barley delivered daily. Cultivated in the Borders, the barley is malted and peated to 30 ppm by Port Ellen Maltings, using peat from Castle Hill on Islay.

The Porteus mill takes 90 minutes to mill each 5.5-tonne batch to the standard industry specification: 20 per cent husk, 70 per cent grits and 10 per cent flour. The mill has an impressive record. Installed in 1963, it has only been repaired once.

There is one name that is synonymous with malt mills: Ronnie Lee. I first saw his name and contact details on a plaque attached to the mill at Lagavulin, so of course I had to call him. Ronnie visits Islay three or four times a year to service mills, and if there is an emergency he can drive from his workshop in South Wales and reach Islay within 10–12 hours. He stocks a large number of spare parts and a number of mills that are undergoing restoration.

All the responsibility for mashing rests on one stainless steel lauter mash tun, with the water supplied by Lochan Sholum. The water is visibly peaty, but this is essentially a visual characteristic; the water doesn't have any phenolic influence.

Ten wooden washbacks are all American larch, and each has a capacity of 21,000 litres (4,600 gallons). Quest distiller's yeast is pitched at 18°C (64°C), with a 55-hour fermentation producing wash at 8% abv.

There are two wash stills and two spirit stills, with four different shapes. The wash stills make me think of an apple and a pear, with slender necks rising above; the two spirit stills are like elongated teardrops, one more curvaceous than the other. The slightly different shape of each spirit still gives the resulting new make spirit a slightly different character. However, new make spirit from both stills is combined, resulting in distinct smoke and peatiness with some apple fruit, and then filled into casks for ageing.

Maturing malt whisky

The filling strength is achieved by diluting the new make spirit with water from Lochan Sholum. The policy is to use second-fill bourbon barrels and bourbon hogsheads, upsized from 200 to 250 litres (44 to 55 gallons), in order to promote the smoky distillery character. Other casks are sourced from Scotch whisky distilleries owned by Diageo. That's hardly a restriction – Diageo owns 29 malt whisky distilleries, including Talisker, Cardhu and Oban; one grain whisky distillery, Cameron Bridge; and has a stake in another grain whisky distillery, North British. Sherry casks are in a minority, but include hogsheads, butts and puncheons.

'At Lagavulin we use refill casks (European oak and American oak), some of which may have been used a few times and will have previously held Scotch. Our focus at Lagavulin is to ensure the distillery character comes through so we can deliver a whisky to the specialist whisky blending team that is in line with the signature smoky character that we all know and love and is iconic to Lagavulin,' says Jordan.

The ageing warehouses at the distillery are all dunnage, accommodating 7,500 casks, with a further 8,000 casks in Port Ellen's ageing warehouses. How long this continues once Port Ellen is operational remains to be seen. Casks are also aged on the mainland in Fife, where malts are married. Around 90 per cent of Lagavulin's production is bottled as a single malt; the youngest of these bottlings are 10 years old. The remaining 10 per cent is used in blended Scotch, notably Johnnie Walker.

Lagavulin tasting notes

Lagavulin 8 year old 48% abv

Nose: Delivery is immediate and giftwrapped: sea breeze and brine suffused with embers, lemon zest, biscotti and really fresh crème caramel top notes.

Palate: Soft mouthfeel; sweetness makes an impressive appearance; toasted and lightly smoky barbecue notes at the core, surrounded by creamy crème caramel, baked apples, toffee and fudge; midway dryness drives the palate with subtle, luscious sweetness wrapped around it, like panna cotta on a spoon.

Finish: Smoke and chargrilled notes rise, with toasted oak, chewy toffee and butterscotch sweetness.

Lagavulin 16 year old 43% abv

Nose: Sea breeze and brine appear together, soon joined by crème brûlée, shortbread and walnuts, with oak adding gravitas. Toasted notes come through at the core.

Palate: Ultra-soft mouthfeel, sweetness balanced by chargrilled notes, served with crème anglaise, lemon meringue and shortbread; then all the flavours embrace each other, sandwiched between a base layer of grilled notes and a top layer of sweetness.

Finish: Mellow oak, crisp, dry, with the edges of the palate garnished by gingerbread and flapjacks, toast and barbecue notes surrounded by sweetness.

Lagavulin 12 year old 56.1% abv (Special Releases 2012)

Nose: Extra-virgin olive oil, then a waft of embers, oak and sea breeze; quite focussed, elegant, fresh and rich.

Palate: Delicate with lovely, luscious lemon, then a waft of toastiness, extra-virgin olive oil and a hint of dry oak, beautifully balanced so that all the flavours come together, on a platform of maltiness.

Finish: Toastiness and dryness lead, then a burst of maltiness.

Lagavulin 12 year old 56.4% abv (Special Releases 2007)

Nose: Honey, gingerbread and rich oak, then top notes of tangerine and orange marmalade, before gingerbread returns to the forefront, accompanied by a waft of smoke.

Palate: Delicate mouthfeel, with balanced richness-dryness immediately opening up, then vanilla sweetness emerges, with a background hint of gentle smoke and toast, then a finale of luscious orange marmalade.

Finish: Dryness leads to juiciness and a delicate waft of smoke.

Lagavulin 21 year old 52% abv (Special Releases 2012)

Nose: Chocolate and vanilla overture, with a gentle waft of smoke bearing oak, while seabreeze includes lemon.

Palate: Elegant mouthfeel, with vanilla sweetness opening proceedings, fresh lemon adds counterpoint, which grows with a hint of maltiness and light oak, mid-way the texture becomes luscious and releases dark chocolate.

Finish: Hint of dryness and maltiness lead, then chocolate and honey add indulgence.

Lagavulin 25 year old, distilled 1977, 57.2% abv

Nose: Pear drops, sherbet and grapefruit provide a constant, with intermittent wafts of caramel, toffee and orange zest, with toasted notes at the edges.

Palate: Crème caramel and grapefruit appear in a delicate but animated texture; hints of vanilla, cocoa powder and liquorice, then culminates in a flourish of crème caramel.

Finish: Crème caramel continues, then hints of toasty smoke and salt.

Chapter Thirteen

Laggan Bay

Chapter Thirteen

Laggan Bay

Who are the Islay Boys? The population is not that large, but without names to go on, where do you start? The Islay Boys aren't a rugby team, or an old school tie network. The Islay Boys is a Scotch whisky bottling company, formed in 2016, which includes an Islay single malt under the brand name Barelegs. There are two Islay boys in the company: Donald MacKenzie from Port Charlotte and Mackay Smith from Portnahaven on Islay's west coast. They are developing a malt whisky distillery, Laggan Bay, in the centre of the island, projected to open in early 2025, with an annual production of 8,000 casks.

'Malt whisky has a very emotional appeal if you're from Islay; it's always there in your life,' explains Donald. The Islay boys are establishing the distillery in partnership with Ian Macleod Distillers, a family company that owns three malt whisky distilleries: Glengoyne in the Highlands, Tamdhu in Speyside and Rosebank in the Lowlands. Donald and Mackay already knew Leonard Russell, the managing director of Ian Macleod Distillers, and the Islay partnership was formed in 2021 over dinner in Deauville. A rendezvous at such a chic location in France sounds extravagant, but was actually a practicality. Leonard was in Deauville on business, thanks to a family interest in racehorses, and Donald lives in Chalo-Saint-Mars, south of Paris.

'We had applied for planning permission to build on a 2.1-hectare site, and knew the style of spirit we wanted to produce. When we told Leonard he said he wanted to be a part of this,' says Donald. 'We had a frank discussion; it was a philosophical meeting of minds. After dinner we stood up, shook hands and that was it. The deal was done.'

The site in Glenegedale by Laggan Bay was found by word of mouth, and an option signed in 2020. This was a relief for Donald and Mackay, as several potential sites for the distillery had previously fallen through. Planning permission for a distillery and one ageing warehouse to store 20,000 casks was granted in 2022, two years after submitting the application. This timescale reflected the Covid-19 pandemic, when the planning department had reduced staffing levels.

Meanwhile, the concept continued to develop. The site is one mile from Laggan Bay, and for ease of reference this was how Donald and Mackay referred to the site. And since Laggan Bay has personal significance for Donald, this provided a name for the distillery. 'Laggan Bay is spectacular and dramatic, a vast curve of sand with a vista out to the west. It's where locals go for a walk on Sunday, where I learned to ride a bike as a wee boy,' says Donald. Laggan Bay is also home to the Big Strand, which at seven miles is Islay's longest beach. But that was never a contender as a name for the distillery. 'Laggan Bay sounds more sonorous than Big Strand, although everyone on Islay will always say I'm going for a walk on Big Strand, not Laggan Bay.'

A tender process for distillery equipment was completed in January 2023. This comprised a mill, one stainless steel mash tun and six stainless steel washbacks, each with a 4-tonne capacity, and a long fermentation is planned; one wash still and one spirit still will be steam-heated, with shell and tube condensers positioned externally.

Finalizing the equipment provided dimensions that were included in the brief for CMA Architects in Glasgow, who also worked on Ardnahoe. As Donald explains: 'We said build an efficient, modern building around the equipment with a big window in the stillhouse. They came up with a stylish version of our original brief, a building that is ecologically and commercially intelligent.'

The design details were finalized at the end of 2022. This included positioning the pot stills against a wall of the stillhouse to maximize the available space. The consequence of this is condensers on the exterior of the stillhouse, which is rarely seen anywhere in Scotland (although Islay has examples at Bowmore and Bunnahabhain). How the ambient temperature, peaking at 17°C (63°F) in summer with a low of 2°C (36°F) in winter, influences the condensers and consequently the character of the new make spirit remains to be seen. Water to cool the condensers will originate from the nearby Glenegedale River, but operate on a closed-loop system (i.e. recycled through a cooling tower and reused).

This is one example of more sustainable, greener production. Another is dealing with spent lees (residue of the second distillation), which is predominantly water, but also contains fats, organic acids, a trace of alcohol, sulphur compounds and copper. The volume is significant: typically one-third of the amount of liquid distilled. Spent lees are usually sent to an effluent plant to be treated. A series of connected reed beds, arranged on a gradient within the distillery grounds, will absorb effluent from the spent lees, while the water will flow forth and return to the source, the Glenegedale River. A case study for this approach is provided by Glengoyne distillery (owned by Laggan Bay's partner, Ian Macleod Distillers), which established reed beds within a wetlands system in 2012. Another benefit of the partnership will be sourcing casks through Ian Macleod Distillers, which has an established supply chain that will ensure choice casks arrive at Laggan Bay.

Chapter Fourteen

Laphroaig

Chapter Fourteen

Laphroaig

'Whisky originated in Ireland, then arrived on Islay, and we perfected it,' said Iain Henderson, who was Laphroaig's distillery manager from 1989–2002. This is quite a claim, but Iain based it on more than his love of Islay. Whisky could have originated in Ireland, on the premise that the knowledge of distilling reached Ireland from China. Distilling was then undertaken in monasteries, which were the earliest centres of learning and science, and distillation was originally used to prepare medicinal remedies. St Columba and Christian missionary monks sailed from Northern Ireland in the sixth century to bring Christianity to Scotland, together with their knowledge of distilling. This is a theory without supporting documentation, but then any records from that era are unlikely to have survived.

However, there is more recent evidence relating to this theory – and an eyewitness in the form of Iain Henderson. The location was Laphroaig distillery, the time was the summer of 1997, which was long and hot, without measurable rainfall for 18 weeks – a record on Islay. In June that year, Iain saw a sailing boat arrive by warehouse no. 1. On closer inspection, the crew was dressed in medieval costumes, and the boat was a replica of a thousand-year-old currach (a traditional Irish boat). The bow had a framework of willow and hazel covered by cowhides and sealed with pitch. The boat had departed from County Mayo in Ireland and was en route to Iona, re-enacting the original route and mode of transport taken by St Columba. Whether St Columba landed on Islay is uncertain, but the fact that this reproduction currach did, before continuing to Mull and Iona, demonstrates that it was possible.

Origins and expressions

Laphroaig's history dates from the early nineteenth century, when two first-generation Ileachs, Donald and Alexander Johnston, leased 1,000 acres from the Laird of Islay in 1810, to raise cattle. They grew barley to feed the cattle, then set up a small distillery to turn surplus barley into whisky. Their father, Alexander, had arrived on Islay in 1745 and acquired a farm.

Donald Johnston was recorded as a distiller by the Excise in 1826, which confirmed his status. Alexander's position was only clarified when he sold his share of the distillery to his brother for £350, then emigrated to Australia. This made Donald the sole owner of Laphroaig in 1836.

Donald's career ended after he fell into a vat of 'burnt ale' (the term then used for pot ale, the residue of the first distillation). Details of this accident may be recorded somewhere, but I decided not to look, as I found this too visceral. Two days later, Donald died. It was 1847: his son Dougald was 11, so his uncle, John Johnston, ran the distillery until 1857, when Dougald took over and continued as the distiller until his death in 1877. His sister, Isabella, had also died, leaving her share of the distillery to her husband, Alexander Johnston, who became the distiller. Alexander's tenure generated sufficient income to rebuild Laphroaig House in 1884, build new stables in 1888 and add no. 3 warehouse in 1889. Part of the income was due to an agreement with neighbouring Lagavulin, under which Laphroaig supplied large amounts of malt whisky to be used in blended Scotch.

Alexander died in 1907, leaving the distillery to his sisters, Mrs William Hunter and Miss Katherine Johnston, and his nephew, Johnston Hunter, who was the chief engineer at Glasgow Tramways. In 1908, Mrs William Hunter's son, Ian Hunter, went to Laphroaig to look after the interests of his mother and aunt. Ian was appointed distillery manager, having trained as an engineer, and he also became involved in the commercial side of the business. When Ian studied the agreement with Lagavulin, he decided that too much Laphroaig was being supplied for blending, and it would be far more profitable to sell this allocation as Laphroaig single malt. With the agreement of Laphroaig's management, he cancelled the agreement. Lagavulin contested this in court and lost. Peter Mackie, who ran Lagavulin, then exacted his revenge by blocking the Kilbride stream with stones, and diverting Laphroaig's water supply. Laphroaig took out a court order to restore the water supply and resumed production.

In 1923, Hunter doubled capacity by adding a new wash and spirit still, and built the malt barns (in their current form). With greater quantities of Laphroaig to sell, Ian also developed export markets, though the USA had become very challenging after Prohibition was ratified in 1919, banning the production and sale of alcohol. The intention was to tackle social problems that the government attributed to alcohol consumption, including of course alcoholism. The only exemption to distil, sell or purchase alcohol was for 'medicinal purposes'. Bourbon, for example, was only available from pharmacies with a doctor's prescription. (I wonder which ailments qualified for this, and the recommended dosage.) Prohibition meant there was only one sales pitch that could work for Laphroaig, and Hunter hailed Laphroaig's phenolic character as 'medicinal'. It worked.

Ian Hunter became the sole owner of Laphroaig in 1926 when his mother and aunt died, and he inherited their share of the distillery. Ian asked his accountant if he knew anyone that could work in the office during the summer of 1933. The accountant had a niece who was looking for a job, having just graduated from Glasgow University. The niece was Bessie Williamson, who arrived on Islay aged 23, intending to return to Glasgow in the autumn and train as a teacher. Bessie's education and logical mind ensured she wasn't an office temp for long. Ian Hunter saw Bessie's potential and started training her for a management role. Laphroaig's management had a lot more to think about when Prohibition in the USA was repealed on 5 December 1933. Laphroaig was no longer confined to pharmacies to alleviate symptoms.

In 1938 Ian suffered a stroke. Confined to a wheelchair, he relied on Bessie and appointed her distillery manager. Bessie had another promotion in 1950 when Ian turned Laphroaig into a private limited company, with himself as managing director, Bessie as director and company secretary and his lawyer, D McCowan Hill, as director. When Ian died in 1954 he left the distillery to Bessie, who became the first woman to own a malt whisky distillery in the twentieth century.

In 1961, Bessie married a Canadian singer-songwriter, Wishart Campbell, who had enchanted her and no doubt serenaded her with his deep, melodic voice. He had retired the previous year from his role as artistic director at a radio station in Toronto, and released an album of his own songs called *A Campbell Comes Home*. This sounds like the soundtrack to living happily ever after on Islay. They were certainly a high-profile couple, driving around Islay in a Triumph Spitfire sports car with purple body work and yellow upholstery. However, some of the song titles from his album began to have additional significance – 'The Mists of Islay', for example, in which Wishart sang that his heart was lost in these mists. Bessie looked for his heart but saw something else, fearing he had fallen in love with her status rather than her. They remained married.

In 1967, Bessie sold Laphroaig to Long John International, a Scottish whisky company, and continued as chairman and director until retiring in 1972.

She remained married until her death in 1982. In her will she left everything to her niece, Helen Powell, and nothing to her husband, who died the following year.

Iain Henderson took over as distillery manager in 1989, having already run ten other distilleries in a long, distinguished career. Iain was also the first distillery manager of Laphroaig that I met. Attending his masterclasses was always memorable. His natural vitality and passion for Laphroaig were very engaging. 'It's in the taste rather than the nose that it's recognizably Laphroaig. Nose the smoke, taste the peat,' he said at the first tasting I attended. His tone was always very personal, and included very amusing anecdotes, and he spoke with knowledge and wisdom gained from his extensive experience.

The following year, Laphroaig was purchased by Allied Domecq, a drinks company that already owned various Scotch whiskies including Ballantine's and Teacher's. Laphroaig grew rapidly during the 1990s, and devotees were able to enjoy a direct connection when The Friends of Laphroaig was formed in 1994. This was publicized by attaching a card to each bottle that served as an application form. Each friend received a square foot of land on Islay, and an invitation to the distillery to collect a dram.

One VIP visitor that year was the then HRH Prince Charles, making his debut at the distillery. It was a memorable visit for various reasons, one of which was that Prince Charles granted Laphroaig a Royal Warrant. This is in recognition of supplying a member of the royal household, initially granted for five years and then reviewed. The Monarch decides who may grant warrants, know as Grantors, which at that time were HM Queen Elizabeth II and Prince Charles. The Royal Warrant also enabled Laphroaig to include the Prince of Wales's feathers on the bottle label. 'I hope you continue to use the traditional methods. I think you make the finest whisky in the world,' wrote Prince Charles, who also holds the title Lord of the Isles, an ancient kingdom that includes Islay (see page 179).

A prime example of traditional methods was the 1960 Vintage Reserve, a 40 year old Laphroaig distilled from Islay-grown barley and malted at the distillery during the reign of Bessie Williamson. She decided to fill European oak sherry casks, rather than the usual bourbon barrels, which matured in warehouse no. 1, the oldest warehouse building. Two hogshead casks were vatted together and filled 300 bottles, half of the original contents having been lost through evaporation. Released in 2001, this was also Laphroaig's oldest expression to date. 'Whilst retaining that uncompromising taste, with a hint of peat and seaweed so distinctive to Laphroaig, this rare 40 year old whisky has a taste reminiscent of sweet liquorice,' said Iain.

In 2002 Iain retired. John Campbell had been Iain's assistant distillery manager since 1999, and continued in this role when Robin Shields was distillery manager from 2003–5. In 2005, Laphroaig was acquired by Jim Beam, which produced the eponymous Jim Beam Bourbon, and in January 2006 John Campbell was appointed distillery manager.

Prior to joining Laphroaig, John had been a lobster fisherman, but being self-employed prevented him from getting a mortgage, and he wanted to buy a house and start a family. John was interviewed by Iain and offered a job in the warehouse team in November 1994, filling casks and sending casks for bottling. 'I had no idea of a career path at Laphroaig,' John says, 'but I soon fell in love with the place. Iain was a good person to learn from: he had drive, enthusiasm and was 100 per cent committed. He treated the business as though it was his own. For me it became more than a job pretty quickly.'

John subsequently worked on the malting floor, then moved to mashing and distilling, and was appointed assistant distillery manager in August 1999. 'When I first started working at the distillery, filling casks in the warehouse, I thought to myself, who's drinking all this Laphroaig? And then as distillery manager I was travelling the world and meeting so many people who loved Laphroaig.'

Creating new expressions is also a vital part of the role. Laphroaig Triple Wood was launched in 2011, and in 2014 a limited-edition 11 year old was released in travel retail (a good reason to go somewhere). This is triple-matured, first in bourbon barrels, then quarter casks and finally Oloroso sherry casks. This was another expression employing 125-litre (27-gallon) quarter casks, which are used as part of the ageing process of Laphroaig Quarter Cask, launched in 2004. This size of cask had its heyday in the early nineteenth century, as a pack horse could manage one on either side of the saddle, but during the nineteenth century they were increasingly regarded as uneconomic. However, these casks contribute a wealth of flavour thanks to the increased surface area contact between the spirit and the oak, creating a creamier, more complex palate.

In 2019, Laphroaig released the first of a series of limited editions celebrating the achievements of Ian Hunter. Five annual releases were planned, with each release featuring a bottle presented within a book that details a chapter in the life and achievements of Ian Hunter. Book One, Unique Character, reflected Ian Hunter's formidable persona. Book Two, Building an Icon, followed in 2020, dedicated to Ian Hunter's tireless commitment to building Laphroaig's profile. Book Three, The Hunter, released in 2021 marked the legacy of the Johnston family to which Ian Hunter belonged. Book Four, Malt Master, in 2022, celebrated the malting floors which Ian established.

John left Laphroaig in November 2021, moving to the mainland to be production director at Lochlea distillery, and was succeeded by Barry MacAffer, an Ileach. 'My family had a long-serving connection with Laphroaig,' Barry explains. 'Growing up on Islay, it was always recognized and seen as the pinnacle of an Islay distillery. We didn't have whisky tourism the way we do now, but the very small number that we did see were always over to visit Laphroaig.'

Barry's grandfather had lived in a distillery house and worked for Ian Hunter and Bessie Williamson. His uncle was an assistant manager. His great aunt, Rachel, saved Ian Hunter from a house fire, who was by then in a wheelchair following the stroke he had suffered, and in gratitude Ian left her a house in his will.

Barry was initially a fisherman on Islay, then decided that was not for him, and qualified as a dental technician in Glasgow. 'Returning to Islay, I worked for the family undertaking business and was saving up to open my own dental lab. Then a job came up at Laphroaig in 2011, and after one week on the malting floor I had forgotten about the dental lab. I loved it,

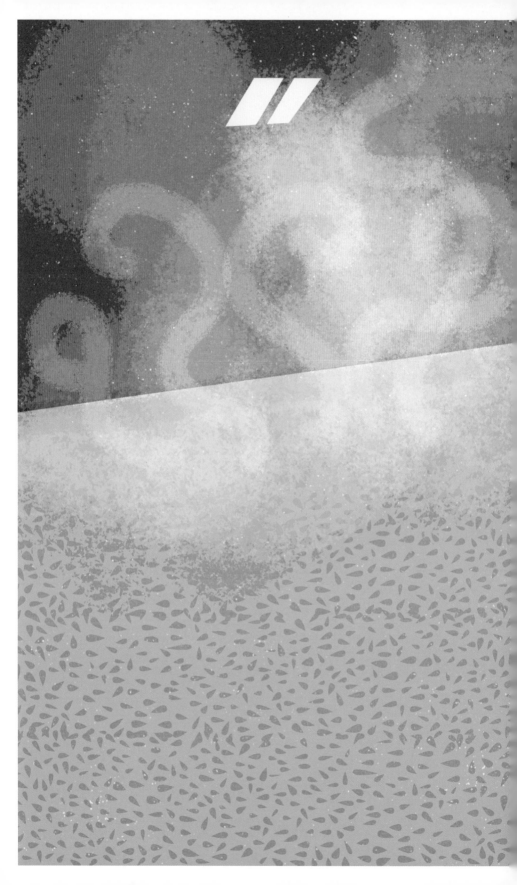

this was the best job I ever had, then I went on to warehousing, and being a mashing and distilling operator.'

Appointed assistant manager in 2015, Barry wanted to challenge himself further, and applied for the job of distillery manager. 'When I got the job, I opened a Laphroaig that had been bottled as a tribute to Bessie Williamson. Bessie was loved and admired by locals; she always opened the doors of Laphroaig for summer fetes and Christmas parties.'

Reflecting on more recent history, Barry continues: 'During lockdown we shut down for nine weeks in the summer of 2020. It was over 30°C on Islay, wildlife took over, cuckoos and woodpeckers could be seen every day at the distillery. When we went back to work, social distancing was straightforward, as each department at Laphroaig is a separate building.'

Spending so much time at home during lockdown was definitely a time to reflect and remember, with an advertising campaign that year having the slogan: 'You'll always remember your first Laphroaig.' I remember mine vividly – the intensity and scale I experienced in my first inhalation amazed me. Whether I liked it or not didn't occur to me, and when I went back for more, I was surprised for a second time. The initial magnificent fanfare of kettledrums, cymbals and double bass had mellowed, and I could hear violins, saxophones and flutes.

Crafting spirit

Barley that is floor-malted and peated at Laphroaig accounts for 20 per cent of the total requirement, while the balance was supplied by Port Ellen Maltings, with various maltsters taking over in 2024. The current variety is Laureate, which was preceded by a familiar sequence of barley varieties, including Optic and Concerto.

Peat is sourced from Glenmachrie, a peat bog six miles from the distillery and owned by Laphroaig for almost 200 years. This is hand-cut annually between March and April, then left to dry and collected in August. Glenmachrie peat comprises mosses, heather, seaweed and grasses, some of which are unique to the island. 'When Islay came out of the sea it brought seaweed with it, so it has a slight marine style. Some people pick up a seaweed, marine-type note. Islay peat gives iodine and salt character,' as Iain Henderson explained.

Peat restoration is a major project for Laphroaig. By 2030, the aim is to restore what is being cut by flooding the land and blocking up ditches, to encourage moss growth.

The steeping regime means barley is under water for 12 hours in cast iron steeps. It is then drained and followed by an equivalent air rest, with another 12 hours of fresh water to reach a 45 per cent moisture level. 'The steeping water is peated, and has an earthy, sulphury note that acts as a glue for the phenolics produced by peating,' says Barry MacAffer.

The malt barns have floor maltings on two storeys, and each floor has a 14-tonne capacity. When the ambient temperature is colder, around 5°C (41°F), the windows are closed and the bed is 20–30 cm (8–12 in) deep to promote the appropriate temperature. In warmer temperatures, around 20°C (68°F), the bed is 15 cm (6 in) deep and the windows are opened. The sensitivity of the barley is such that even strong sunlight shining through a window can create a hot spot in which barley germinates more rapidly.

Two neighbouring kilns are used to peat and dry. The malt is spread using a device that propels barley across the floor of the kiln. The fire is started using wood from pallets, then peat is piled on – initially dry peat, which produces slightly less smoke but creates a good heat in the fire that helps to get the most from the wetter peat. The steam this creates acts as a vehicle for flavour compounds. Steam and smoke rise towards the barley 4.5 metres (15 feet) above, with a Doig Ventilator in the roof drawing smoke through more effectively. Powdered peat is used to create more smoke towards the end of the run, which takes 12–18 hours depending on the time of year and the age of the peat. Every week, 4 tonnes of peat are used to achieve a peating level of more than 65 ppm.

'A lot of medicinal notes come from sphagnum moss, but this depends more on the way you burn it. We use a cold-smoking process, with a maximum temperature of about 20°C. This produces a different result to hot smoking, with oily creosols and medicinal guaiacols in different levels compared to warm-smoked. Some people perceive seaweed, and a marine note,' says Barry MacAffer.

The peated malt is subsequently dried for 12 hours, reducing the moisture level to 4.5 per cent using hot air. This is generated by passing air between radiators heated by hot water.

The Porteus mill, in a characteristic shade of red, dates from 1984, and the resulting grist is 70 per cent grits, 20 per cent husk and 10 per cent fines. The objective of mashing is a clear wort in order to promote fruitiness.

Fermentation is 72 hours in eight stainless steel washbacks, with the wort at 18–20°C (64–68°F) when pitching Mauri or Quest yeast (the variety is said to make no difference). The resulting wash is 8.5% abv.

Onion-shaped wash and spirit stills are heated using steam coils that have additional cylinders attached, extending the surface area contact with the liquid and giving more control over the rate of distillation. The fourth spirit still, which has twice the capacity of the other three, is affectionately known as 'Bessie', having been purchased by Bessie Williamson. Demand for Laphroaig had been growing and Bessie decided to increase production. Her plan was to add two more spirit stills that matched the others. However, Bessie's budget wasn't quite enough. But the budget was enough to purchase one larger still, which proved to be less expensive than two smaller stills.

The foreshots are the longest on Islay, possibly Scotland, and the spirit cut extends for longer than other Islay distilleries. The objective is to capture the peaty, medicinal, tar notes that come through later in the distillation run.

The new make spirit includes peaty, earthy, smoky bonfire on the beach notes, balanced by the sweetness of ripe fruit. By this stage the peating level is 15 ppm, down from the original 45 ppm. New make spirit from all the stills is blended together for ageing.

Maturing malt whisky

The distillation strength of 68% abv is reduced to the filling strength of 63.5% abv using water from the Kilbride stream, which has a peaty tint and a peating level of 1.5 ppm.

Historically, sherry and wine casks were used for maturation, with bourbon barrels pioneered by Ian Hunter. This approach has continued, as bourbon barrels, all first fill, account for 96 per cent of the cask inventory. And 95 per cent of the bourbon barrels are supplied by Maker's Mark with the same charring level, classified as a number 3 (see page 49). This is the result of charring for 40 seconds, which opens up the pores, caramelizes the sugars in the oak and produces vanillin (which gives vanilla notes). Laphroaig and Maker's Mark are both owned by Beam Suntory, a multinational with a broad portfolio of bourbon, Scotch, Japanese and Irish whiskies, so an intercompany arrangement is completely logical.

Ageing Laphroaig in bourbon barrels shows phenolics from the new make spirit more clearly than sherry casks. Laphroaig uses Spanish oak, Oloroso and Pedro Ximénez casks, with Laphroaig 30 year old, for example, aged exclusively in sherry casks.

The impact of phenolics is also determined by the length of ageing. Up to 20 years, the peat and smoke are in the foreground but balanced by other characteristics. From 30–40 years, peat and smoke move into the background.

Laphroaig is matured on Islay in six warehouses. Three are racked, storing casks 11 high. One is part-dunnage and part-racked. Two are dunnage, stacking barrels two to three high. No. 1 warehouse has walls 60 cm (2 ft) thick, and a seafront location, with the temperature throughout the year around 7–8°C (45--46°F), feeling cool in summer and warm in winter. What a perfect haven from the weather, with plenty of refreshments available.

Laphroaig tasting notes

Laphroaig 10 year old 40% abv

Nose: Creosote and burned embers, from which vanilla custard and lemon zest gradually emerge, then the focus moves to crème caramel, extra-virgin olive oil and burned toast.

Palate: Light, elegant mouthfeel, with lusciously creamy lemon meringue expanding across the palate, garnished by lemon zest and wafting smoke; underlying chargrilled notes and lusciously sweet top notes, which meet and meld in the middle of the palate.

Finish: Light dryness begins, then toasted, barbecued notes grow and overlay the dryness.

Laphroaig Select 40% abv

Nose: Elegant freshness, lemon syllabub laced with smoke, baked apples, cloves and a lightly earthy garnish with lemon zest.

Palate: Lightly velvety mouthfeel with lemon zest that soon intertwines with smoky toastiness evolving into barbecued notes, joined by subtle maltiness and cider. Gentle underlying dryness is overlain by lusciousness and extends across the entire palate. Retains composure while gaining depth.

Finish: Light dryness, then shortbread sweetness opens up with light creaminess and aniseed, culminating in tangy dryness.

Laphroaig Quarter Cask 48% abv

Nose: Animated aromas race to the nose; toastiness and smoke meld with top notes of coconut, nutmeg, milk chocolate and shortbread.

Palate: Silky mouthfeel, composed and generous flavours flow, with creamy coconut and underlying shortbread; indulgent sweetness with a hint of honey and crème caramel, then sweetness and dryness rotate around each other, animating the flavour profile.

Finish: Light dryness is soon joined by creamy lemon meringue sweetness and thick set honey.

Laphroaig 10 year old 40% abv

Nose: Lovely medley of embers, peat and smoky vanilla with a garnish of TCP, salty lemon, sea spray and smoky, cooked fruit.

Palate: Delicate softness, but with real range as well as elegance; delicious, smoky, fruity, vanilla pod and vanilla crème anglaise, tarte tatin and salty lemon; rich-dry interplay, with espresso, dark chocolate, malty, digestive biscuit notes emerging.

Finish: Rich, dry finish with a sea spray smokiness and bonfire on the beach.

Laphroaig Lore 48% abv

Nose: Earthy, embers, barbecued notes that turn medicinal with a hint of Germolene; then another movement sees the sudden appearance of vanilla, with underlying toastiness. Rich and elegant.

Palate: Smoke rises from toast, enriched by earthiness, then some sweetness emerges with a wave of juicy oranges and lemons garnished with the freshness of lemon zest, while underlying oak dryness adds emphasis.

Finish: Initial light dryness extends with lightly earthy, toasted notes.

Laphroaig 1960, 40 year old, cask strength 42.4% abv

Nose: Focussed brine and smoke, an inhalation of sea air, then lemon freshness and vanilla indulgence; carbolic soap has a moment in the spotlight before bowing out to oak, vanilla and a hint of toast.

Palate: Incredibly elegant mouthfeel and delivery; smoke, vanilla and fruit cake open up, then baked apples, honey and cloves emerge, with creamy, malty, digestive biscuit notes, a hint of sweet oranges, salt and lemons.

Finish: Smoke mingles with fresh lemon and culminates in dark chocolate.

Chapter Fifteen

Port Ellen

Chapter Fifteen

Port Ellen

When a distillery ceases production and closes, silence is all that exists beyond locked doors. The past can be recalled, but there is no future. It's the end of an era. And that's how it seemed when Port Ellen closed in 1983. Port Ellen was essentially a component of blended Scotch such as Johnnie Walker, and sales of blends had seriously declined, resulting in what was termed the 'whisky loch'. Substantial reserves of malt and grain whisky had been made redundant, robbed of their traditional role in life. And the end of this era only served to underline the end of Port Ellen.

But another era began when Port Ellen's distinctive, heavily peated style became more appreciated, and its appeal was intensified by the rarity. This reappraisal was all the more extraordinary considering that Port Ellen didn't have such a following while operational. There is only one known instance of a proprietary bottling of Port Ellen, and its individuality could hardly be appreciated when part of a blended Scotch. Otherwise, Port Ellen was only available as a single malt from independent bottlers such as Gordon & MacPhail, on an ad hoc basis.

Some of us hoped that one day Port Ellen might reopen. I asked the right people at Diageo about this a number of times. Their replies didn't encourage me, but I remained optimistic. And then the news came through: Port Ellen was going to reopen.

Origins and expressions

Port Ellen's origins were a malt mill in the town of Port Ellen, which was repurposed into a distillery in 1824 by A K Mackay & Co. The distillery was innovative from the beginning: a spirit safe was first tested at Port Ellen distillery in the winter of 1824, and subsequently became a standard feature in all malt whisky distilleries. This was prompted by the 1823 Excise Act: a padlocked spirit safe with a key held by the Excise officer stationed at the distillery ensured excise was paid on all spirit produced.

A K Mackay & Co. declared bankruptcy, but this created an opportunity for John Ramsay to take a lease on the distillery in 1836, aged 21. He had already learned the art of distilling, having been sponsored by an uncle to go to Alloa, a town in the Central Lowlands, where another relative was a perfect mentor for such a protégé. This was Robert Stein, who was born into a family of distillers and distillery owners and owned Kilbagie distillery. But Robert wasn't someone to simply sit back and spend his income. He was also an inventor, having developed a patent still in 1826, and so had plenty of knowledge to pass on to John.

The patent still had an amazing impact. Being a less expensive, more efficient means of distilling grain whisky, it led to another innovation: blending grain whisky with malt whisky and creating a new style, blended Scotch. John Ramsay also experimented with a patent still between 1841–3, but not to distil grain whisky; he wanted to explore the results of distilling malt whisky in this way. His verdict on this experiment isn't recorded, but as it was short-lived it (presumably) didn't achieve what he was looking for. It exemplifies, however, his inquisitive, pioneering nature.

Another example of this is that John Ramsay was exporting significant quantities of Port Ellen single malt to the USA as early as 1840 (confirmed by archival records). He consolidated this in 1848 by negotiating the rights to store casks in bonded warehouses prior to exporting. This meant that he could defer paying duty until the casks actually left the warehouse and were bound for the USA. Archive records also show that John Ramsay imported sherry and Madeira casks in which to mature his spirit.

In 1848, John Ramsay purchased the Kildalton Estate on Islay, the principal residence being a stone mansion set in a deer park, as well as a dower house and various cottages. The estate extended to 54,500 acres across much of southern Islay, including the Port Ellen distillery and many houses in the town of Port Ellen, together with 45 farms.

John's political ambitions saw him elected MP for Stirling when a by-election (special election) was held in 1868. Later that year a general election was called and he lost his seat. But he gained a commercial ally in W P Lowrie, a Scotch whisky blender and broker who took over sales of Port Ellen in 1869. This must have allowed John Ramsay to spend more time on his political ambitions. In 1874 he was elected MP for Falkirk, a post he held until 1886.

Meanwhile, Ramsay had also become joint owner of the SS *Islay* in 1876, which began sailing between Port Ellen and Port Askaig on Islay to Glasgow, taking passengers and cargo. He died in 1892, and relatives inherited his substantial assets. In 1920, the Ramsay family sold the distillery to Port Ellen Distilling Company, which had been formed by two Scotch whisky barons, James Buchanan and John Dewar. They subsequently acquired the Lowrie Company, and so controlled sales rights as well as production. In 1930, Port Ellen was amalgamated into this larger company. But once part of a larger portfolio of distilleries, it was decided that Port Ellen was no longer needed. The distillery buildings were largely demolished in the 1930s.

In 1960, a decision was taken to rebuild the distillery, presumably due to optimism about the future of blended Scotch. The premises were refurbished with new equipment, and Port Ellen was operational in 1967. The stills were direct-fired until 1970, when steam coils were introduced. The floor maltings closed in 1973, when the purpose-built Port Ellen Maltings opened a short distance away.

A very special visitor in 1980 was HM Queen Elizabeth II, whose visit was marked by a special bottling, Port Ellen 12 year old, Queen's visit 1980. Each person present during the royal visit received a bottle, and it is thought a total of 40 bottles were produced. The distillery closed in 1983, and of the existing workforce, 28 were transferred to Port Ellen Maltings and 17 were made redundant.

Port Ellen was only available as a single malt from independent bottlers such as Samaroli in Italy, with a 23 year old distilled in 1975 being released in 1992. Port Ellen began to be available as a proprietary bottling in the Rare Malts annual releases, which ran between 1995–2005. Port Ellen 20 year old distilled in 1978, bottled at a cask strength of 60.9% abv, was released in 1998. A 24 year old distilled in 1978, bottled at a cask strength of 59.35% abv, was released in 2002, with 12,000 bottles priced at £110 each. In 2004, a 24 and a 25 year old Port Ellen were released.

The Rare Malts series evolved into Special Releases in 2005, which included a Port Ellen 22 year old distilled in 1978 at a cask strength of 56.2% abv, together with two expressions of Talisker. The applause this initial trio received led to an annual release of several rare, limited-edition malts at cask strength from distilleries owned by Diageo. The line-up varied, but Port Ellen, together with Caol Ila and Lagavulin, made regular appearances.

Special Releases soon became an annual highlight for many whisky lovers, whether purchasing to collect and possess, or to savour the contents. Attending the press preview each year was an opportunity to taste each bottling, and talk to distillery managers as well as master blenders who manned tables and poured for us. This included such luminaries as Dr Jim Beveridge OBE, who retired in 2021 having been Johnnie Walker's master blender, and Maureen Robinson, one of the first women to hold the title of master blender, who retired in 2020 after an exemplary 45-year career in Scotch whisky. This really heightened the experience, as I could ask what it was about a particular malt whisky that led to it being selected.

I always tasted the Port Ellen last, partly due to practicality since it was the most phenolic, so tasting anything after that would be garnished with Port Ellen; but also because it was always my favourite, and I wanted it to be the culmination of the tasting. The Port Ellen malts bottled for this series were distilled between 1967–83, which turned out to be a magnificent era yielding some exceptional examples.

In 2017, it was announced that Port Ellen distillery would be restored and reopened. Diageo was able to draw on an extensive archive containing architectural drawings, leases and other documentation. The only surviving buildings were the kiln, with its classic pagoda roofs, an original office block and several seafront dunnage warehouses, also in need of restoration. The existing equipment had been removed and relocated to other distilleries after Port Ellen closed in 1983.

A large new stillhouse provides stylish accommodation, with large picture windows providing great views of the interiors from the exterior, and vice versa. The stillhouse has two pairs of pot stills, with each pair doing its own thing. One pair follows a traditional distillation regime, replicating Port Ellen's original new make spirit character. The other pair of pot stills is smaller, and free to experiment and produce different styles of new make spirit. It's a great combination of the familiar and the unexpected.

The restoration project was led by Alexander McDonald from 2021, and he was subsequently appointed distillery manager in 2022. A native of Argyll, born and brought up in Lochgilphead, Alexander qualified at the Institute of Brewing & Distilling and has lived on Islay since 2014. Initially he worked at Kilchoman distillery, and was then appointed distiller at Caol Ila and Lagavulin. 'It is an honour and a privilege to be appointed as Port Ellen distillery manager. This is an incredibly exciting time for everyone at Port Ellen and I look forward to leading the team as we prepare for the historic moment when spirit flows through the stills once again,' said Alexander.

Work restarted on Port Ellen in October 2021, following a pause in construction due to Covid-19. Distilling was due to begin in 2023. While the world waits for Port Ellen to become operational, only a finite amount of original stock remains.

Meanwhile, Port Ellen contributed to the first private-label, single-cask whisky from dekantā (which holds the world's largest online inventory of Japanese whisky). Eigashima 2011 The Kikou–Ki Series, bottled at 58.4% abv, was finished in a freshly emptied Port Ellen cask, yielding 300 bottles released in 2018. The resulting whisky spans seaweed, beach bonfire, lemon sherbet and citrus aromas, with a hint of earthiness, embers and roasted coffee beans on the palate.

The Eigashima distillery is less than 100 metres (110 yards) from the Harima-nada sea, the closest whisky distillery to the coast in Japan, and this is reflected in the savoury, saline distillery character. A family-owned distillery and the first to be granted a licence to produce Japanese whisky in 1919, Eigashima is Japan's smallest whisky producer, with a team of just five people.

Auction prices are always interesting to read, and a good indication (but not a guarantee) of the value of rare Islay bottlings. The Port Ellen 12 year old, Queen's Visit 1980 achieved a hammer price of £100,000 on Whisky Auctioneer on 6 June 2022. A week later, another example of Port Ellen was auctioned by Sotheby's in London: a 43 year old cask that achieved £875,000 on 14 June 2022. The cask was no. 1145, filled with new make spirit in 1979 reaching a cask strength of 52.9% abv, with a yield of approximately 102 bottles at cask strength. The purchase price included a visit to Islay and a private tour of the Port Ellen distillery, together with a sculpture in coloured Murano glass representing the 'Dram and the Water', created by artist and designer Ini Archibong.

Port Ellen now has a present and a future, in addition to its past, which qualifies it as a historic malt whisky landmark, not far from another historic monument, the Carraig Fhada lighthouse at the entrance to Port Ellen bay. This was built by the Laird of Islay, Walter Frederick Campbell, in 1832, to commemorate his wife, Lady Eleanor, who died that year aged 36. The unusual design of the lighthouse, which is square and resembles the turret of a castle with crenellations, is thought to be the only example of its kind in Scotland.

Port Ellen tasting notes

Port Ellen 28 year old distilled 1979, 53.8% abv (Special Releases 2007)

Nose: Waft of toastiness, hint of creosote, oak, then vanilla emerges, followed by cappuccino garnished with cocoa powder.

Palate: Ultra-delicate mouthfeel; creamy crème caramel, chocolate, zesty lemon with underlying dryness and a gentle waft of lightly smoky, toasted notes, culminating in dark chocolate and sweetness.

Finish: Toasty, lightly smoky, with dryness building.

Port Ellen 32 year old distilled 1979, 52.5% abv (Special Releases 2012)

Nose: Olive oil, sea breeze, vanilla and honey, then lovely soft ripe fruit, baked apples, hints of apricot and orange marmalade.

Palate: Delicate, elegant, lovely ripe fruitiness opens up, apples, apricots, orange marmalade, hint of oak and mellow background waft of smoke, more elegant fruitiness and a hint of honey, cloves and cinnamon.

Finish: Dryness, maltiness, then honey and fruit emerge.

Portintruan

Chapter Sixteen

Portintruan

What does it take to open a distillery? Funding and commercial acumen, of course, but also knowledge, experience and a passion for whisky. Two brothers, Sukhinder and Rajbir Singh, each have these credentials, which means that together they have double what is needed to make a success of Portintruan (pronounced *Port-nah-truan*). Named after the historic farm estate where the distillery is located, and meaning 'place of the stream', the distillery is projected to open in 2024.

The brothers opened The Whisky Exchange in 1999, which was rapidly established as a global whisky headquarters, retailing an extensive range of Scotch whisky (not to mention every other style of whisky). The Whisky Exchange also makes dreams come true for collectors and whisky lovers by listing expressions no longer in production, and therefore all the more desirable.

I first met Sukhinder when we were both invited to visit Auchentoshan Distillery just outside Glasgow. After checking out the distillery, we went into an ageing warehouse and sampled several casks, discussing which we liked most. These samples were sufficient to send me into a malt whisky wonderland, and then we headed into Glasgow to tour the whisky bars. We talked Scotch whisky, and he spoke with great insight and authority, but also with humour and charm.

After our Glasgow trip I saw Sukhinder at various tastings, sometimes with Raj, and sometimes Raj without Sukhinder. Whenever a limited edition was launched I used to tell the brand owners, 'Why don't you just give the entire allocation to Sukhinder? He'll sell it all.' When Sukhinder and Raj launched the Whisky Show in London in 2008 it was an immediate success, with an amazing range of malts to sample. The Whisky Show continues to be an annual highlight of the whisky calendar, and the opening of Portintruan will be another special event.

'We've worked closely with the Argyll and Bute planning committee to create plans for a distillery that fits into the landscape and supports the community. We want to create whiskies that inspire both the people of Islay and Islay whisky fans worldwide, enhancing the already glowing reputation of Islay whiskies, while also becoming an integral part of the community,' says Sukhinder.

Crafting spirit

Located between Port Ellen distillery and Laphroaig, the foundations of Portintruan were laid in 2022, with the steel structure for the buildings in position in the spring of 2023. The layout includes floor maltings with automated turners that move along the malting floor and kiln. A beam on runners fixed to the walls is equipped with rotating 'ploughs'. Peating times vary from 8 to 16 hours to provide a range of peating levels, followed by hot air to dry the barley. The process of blending is used (blending peated with unpeated malt), as this is a more accurate method of achieving particular peating levels. The floor maltings are able to supply more than 50 per cent of the production capacity, which is 1 million litres (220,000 gallons) per annum.

'With a new distillery we can create whatever we want, and we have a bespoke system to make traditional flavour-led whiskies using modern technology as well as hands-on processes to help create those flavours,' says Georgie Crawford, who was appointed Portintruan's distillery manager in 2020. Raised on Islay, Georgie began her career on the mainland, at the Scotch Malt Whisky Society in Edinburgh, later moving into site operations at Glen Ord and Teaninich. In 2010, Georgie returned to Islay to be the first female distillery manager at Lagavulin. Plans to reopen Port Ellen distillery led to Georgie being appointed the project implementation manager in 2018. Meanwhile, she had also been friends with Sukhinder for many years.

Portintruan's equipment, installed in the autumn of 2023, comprises a semi-lauter mash tun and stainless steel as well as wooden washbacks produced by JB Vats. Building work continued around the equipment, allowing a further year to complete pipework and electrics. 'Different production regimes were mapped out in advance in order to distil new make spirits with different peating levels and flavour profiles. Being able to move seamlessly from producing one style of malt to another is the challenge,' says Georgie.

A 120-hour fermentation is intended to produce a rich, fruity wash. The wash still is direct-fired, a rarity in Scotland and unique on Islay. Heat is provided by a furnace beneath the pot, resembling a burner in a domestic boiler. Controlling the size of the flame is simply a case of opening or closing a valve, which is automated. As the level of heat is intense, the interior of the still is fitted with a rummager, a rotating chain that 'scrapes' the base of the still, preventing the wash from baking onto the surface.

'Direct firing produces a complex, almost caramelized effect, which adds a different depth of flavour,' Georgie continues. The spirit still is heated using steam coils, with the lyne arm extending slightly upwards to increase reflux. The lyne arm is also fitted with a purifier (a cooling jacket through which cold water circulates) to provide further reflux, with the condensate directed back into the still for redistillation.

'We will be producing four or five new make spirits, with varying phenol levels and different spirit cuts, which means the feints will vary depending on each spirit cut. So we will have multiple feints vessels to isolate the feints from each expression. This means the parameters for ageing are incredible,' Georgie explains. Shell and tube condensers use water on a loop passing through a cooling tower, which minimizes the amount of water needed.

Portintruan is unusual in having another, separate pilot distillery with all its own equipment: a hammer mill that can deal with any grain, while stainless steel washbacks will include temperature-controlled jackets; a wash still and a spirit still, accompanied by a column still and a retort (a copper pot filled with weak distillate through which the vapours pass, and with which they interact, creating a different influence). Any combination and permutation of these stills can be employed, with the option of distilling wash from the main distillery to see how this behaves during different distillation regimes.

Facilities include a visitor space, bar and restaurant, and although Portintruan malt whisky won't be served for a good few years, two Islay brands, Port Askaig and Elements of Islay (already bottled by Elixir Distillers), will be available. A multipurpose educational facility with a sensory lab and classroom will offer opportunities for research and experimentation, for local people as well as industry professionals. There is also the intention of creating an apprentice programme to train the next generation of distillers. I will definitely be applying!

Independent bottlers & cask influences

Chapter Seventeen

Independent bottlers & cask influences

Does it seem ironic that the greatest source of Islay malts always used to be independent bottlers rather than the distilleries that produced them? Independent bottlers have a long tradition of buying casks of malt whisky and bottling the contents under their own label, often in conjunction with the name of the distillery (depending on the agreement between both parties). For distilleries this was a sales channel generating additional income. For independent bottlers, some of which were originally wine merchants or grocers, malt whisky was an additional item to offer their clientele.

Independent bottlers such as Gordon & MacPhail, A D Rattray, Duncan Taylor and Signatory are all based in Scotland, along with Berry Bros & Rudd in London. The first independent bottler of Scotch whisky that wasn't in England or Scotland was Samaroli in Italy, where appreciation of malt whisky was at a more advanced level. Silvano Samaroli (1939–2017) established his eponymous company in Rome in 1968, initially importing malts and from 1979 bottling malts under the company's own label. During the 1980s he began to bottle cask-strength malts, which was an innovation at that time. Casks of Islay malt were readily available, but that doesn't detract from Silvano's superlative cask selection. Silvano also produced artistic, innovative labels and drew the group of bright red carnations on the Flowers series of bottlings himself.

Samaroli Bowmore Bouquet 1966, bottled in 1984, is regarded as one of the finest malt whiskies ever bottled, with only 720 bottles released. When a bottle was auctioned in 2014 it made £4,200, and in 2022 an online auction held by Perth-based company Whisky Auctioneer saw it achieve £51,611. Similarly, Samaroli Laphroaig 1967 Sherry Wood 15 year old was a release of 720 bottles in 1982. One bottle, auctioned in 2014, achieved £5,700. Another, signed by Silvano Samaroli, was sold by Whisky Auctioneer in 2018 for £61,000.

Blended and branded Islay malts

A name that indicates the flavour and persona of a malt whisky, while also having a sense of humour, is definitely a high achiever. Peat Monster is such a name, and its creator was Compass Box, an independent bottler based in London. Making its debut in 2003, the objective for Peat Monster was to balance fruit flavours with heavy peat by blending malt from Caol Ila with heavily peated malt from Ardmore in the Highlands. Peat Monster is also an interesting case study, the recipe having been revised in 2008 for its fifth anniversary.

'We decided to up the peating level by adding malt from the Laphroaig distillery. We also added a tiny amount of malt aged in French oak casks to add sweetness. We tried the recipe with and without this, and even adding 1 per cent enhanced the flavour,' says John Glaser, founder of Compass Box.

The Peat Monster recipe was revisited again in 2018, to see how it compared with the growing number and range of peated malts. 'To make sure Peat Monster delivered, we increased the age of the malts from the Caol Ila and Laphroaig distilleries from 10 to 13 years. Using malts that are three or more years older than their predecessors makes a noticeable difference. There is now more appreciation for peated malts with balance and elegance.'

While John readily reveals component malts in Peat Monster, a mystery surrounds Smokehead. 'We've never told anyone where the Smokehead whisky actually comes from on Islay. It is fascinating for fans not to know; they enjoy speculating, discussing and arguing,' says Iain Weir, brand director of Ian Macleod Distillers, which produces Smokehead. If anyone thinks they know the source of Smokehead, they should also know something else. 'Smokehead has always been a single malt. We've used single malt from different Islay distilleries over the years, but always maintained the same flavour profile and characteristics: smoky, peaty, phenolic. Opening a bottle of Smokehead, you are immediately hit by medicinal Islay notes and a lovely honeyed sweetness; it's definitely not one dimensional and this was always our intention.'

The role of Islay malts in blended Scotch

Is it regrettable when a favourite malt is part of a blended Scotch, and becomes part of a group number rather than a solo performer? Of course not! This is another way of enjoying a malt; it may not be individually discernible, but it's there. And isn't it preferable to drink a blend with, rather than without, your favourite malt?

The recipe of a blended Scotch can contain various malt and grain whiskies from various distilleries and of various ages. A higher percentage of malts and older malts does not in itself guarantee greater complexity. This is created by interaction and balance between component whiskies. Interaction is a fascinating process, with some flavours promoted, others relegated.

'We were experimenting with a known blend without any peated malt, and it was lovely, but not as fruity or as open as we wanted or expected. Adding a little peated malt opened everything up, and it became more exuberant and flavourful,' says Emma Walker, master blender at Johnnie Walker. This doesn't mean that adding peated malts automatically elevates a blend – it is the master blender's skill and judgement that achieves this.

'Used in the right proportions, smoke brings everything to a pinnacle, dialling up the volume and helping to bridge flavours. But too much smoke can drown out other flavours and add ashy notes,' Emma explains.

Peated malts can also make a valid contribution to a blend while remaining anonymous. 'Adding peated malts to a blend isn't always about discernible smoke, as smoke can do very clever things without being visible. It can lengthen mouthfeel, emphasize sweetness and influence flavours, for example making milk chocolate notes taste a little more like dark chocolate,' says Emma.

Islay malts have always played an important role in various Johnnie Walker expressions. When Caol Ila and Lagavulin appear together in a blend, as in Johnnie Walker Black Label Islay Origin, there is a fascinating interaction. 'Caol Ila has a wood smoke with lovely sweetness, while Lagavulin has more medicinal smoke. Some components are identical in both malts while others are different, so some phenolics reinforce each other, while others make an individual contribution adding range to a blend,' explains Emma.

Islay's additional influence

How can an unpeated malt whisky gain phenolic character? The Balvenie is a classic example of how elegant a Speyside malt can be, serving up vanilla and honey, though The Balvenie Islay Cask 17 year old featured an additional characteristic. A parcel of 17 year old Balvenie was filled into 94 casks that had previously been used to age a peated Islay malt. Although casks are empty when sold, the staves remain saturated by the previous occupant. When the casks were filled with Balvenie, this residue left the staves and integrated into the malt. After six months, David Stewart, The Balvenie's malt master, decided the delicate peatiness and smoky sweetness the casks had contributed was just right. Released in 2001, this approach was a revelation. I loved the elegance and richness, with creamy vanilla and underlying wafts of smoke, apricots, honey and a subtle citrus garnish. David continued his extraordinary creativity, and in 2022, by then the recipient of an MBE, he celebrated his 60th anniversary at The Balvenie.

Another major event in 2022 was the release of Ploughing Edition, an unpeated malt distilled by Lochlea distillery in the Lowlands of Scotland, which was fully matured in quarter casks previously used to age a peated Islay malt. The starting point, Lochlea's new make spirit, has upfront fruit, green apples and pears, then grassy, cereal and biscuit notes. 'You have to deliver two profiles, Lochlea and peat. Ploughing Edition is Lochlea in a bubble of Islay peat. Fruit notes and sweetness come through first, then a lot of peat smoke comes through at the back end of the palate,' says John Campbell, Lochlea's production director.

Gazetteer

Every distillery on Islay has a visitor centre offering very welcome and fulfilling retail opportunities, including expressions that are distillery exclusives and only available there and then, as well as branded clothing and, increasingly, local arts and crafts. Below are a few additional suggestions when spending time on Islay.

The Islay Hotel in the town of Port Ellen is walking distance from Port Ellen distillery and Port Ellen Maltings, and has wonderful views over the bay of Port Ellen. There is also a great view in the bar, which has plenty of Islay malts to enjoy and great food to order.

CHARLOTTE STREET, PORT ELLEN, PA42 7DF. THEISLAYHOTEL.COM

The Bowmore Hotel has two bars full of Islay malts, and display cases in other parts of the hotel that are an archive to be treasured.

JAMIESON STREET, BOWMORE, PA43 7HL. BOWMOREHOTEL.CO.UK

The Celtic House bookshop and cafe has a great selection of books on Islay and on Scotch whisky. I can never walk past a bookshop without going in, and as I love coffee and cakes, I can then make my way to the en suite cafe.

SHORE STREET, BOWMORE, PA43 7LD. WWW.THECELTICHOUSE.CO.UK

The Islay Malt Whisky Academy was founded by Rachel MacNeil, who began writing about malt whisky as a hobby on her website in 2009. In 2015, Rachel ran her first one-week whisky course on Islay, and also offers online and residential courses. Combining knowledge with passion and charm, Rachel provides the equivalent of an Oxbridge education in Islay malts.

17 BROOMHILL, BOWMORE, PA43 7HX. ISLAYWHISKYACADEMY.SCOT

Glossary

Barley husk: the outer surface of the barley grain.

Bere barley: a historic variety of barley, considered the 'original'.

Draff: the grist remaining in the mash tun once mashing is completed.

Filling strength: the alcoholic strength of the new make spirit when it is filled into a cask.

Heads or foreshots: the initial phase of the second distillation.

Low wines: the result of the first distillation.

Lyne arm: a copper pipe that conducts vapours from the top of the still to the condenser.

Malt mill: Where barley is milled in order to begin the production process.

Mash tun: a stainless steel vessel in which mashing takes place, converting starches into sugars and rinsing phenolics from the grain.

    Lauter mash tun: a mash tun equipped with a rotating arm that can also be raised and lowered.

    Semi-lauter mash tun: a mash tun equipped with a rotating arm.

New make spirit: freshly distilled spirit ready to be filled into casks for ageing.

Phenolics: the overall term for phenolic compounds such as phenol, guaiacol and cresol.

Sparge: the final batch of water during mashing, recycled as the first water of the subsequent mashing cycle.

Spirit cut: the second phase of the second distillation, which is reserved as the new make spirit.

Spirit still: undertakes the second distillation.

Tails or feints: the final phase of the second distillation.

Wash: alcoholic liquid produced by fermentation, ready to be distilled.

Wash still: undertakes the first distillation.

Washbacks: wooden or stainless steel vessels in which the wort is fermented.

Wort: the sweet, phenolic liquid that is the result of mashing.

Farewell Islay!

Finishing this book marked the end of an intense and fulfilling phase of researching, thinking and writing about Islay and Islay malts. It was a phase I greatly enjoyed, and which I missed as soon as it was over. I'm very grateful to everyone I met at each distillery for giving me such a warm welcome, and for sharing their knowledge so generously. When I next go to Islay there will be many familiar places and processes, but there will also be new developments for me to explore, and always more for me to learn. There are also endless panoramas to appreciate, wherever I am on the island, and I'll continue to marvel at the romance and beauty of this very special place.

I would like to thank the following people for sharing their knowledge and experience so generously: Colin Gordon, Dr Bill Lumsden and Jackie Thomson at Ardbeg; Fraser Hughes, Ardnahoe; David Turner, Bowmore; Andrew Brown and Brendan McCarron at Bunnahabhain; Adam Hannett, Bruichladdich; Samuel Hale, Caol Ila; Bertram Nesselrode, ili; Anthony Wills and Derek Scott at Kilchoman; Jordan Paisley, Lagavulin; Donald MacKenzie, Laggan Bay; Barry MacAffer, Laphroaig; Georgie Crawford, Portintruan; James Brown, Octomore Farm; John Glaser, Compass Box; John Campbell, Lochlea; Emma Walker, Johnnie Walker Blended Scotch; Barry Harrison, John Conner and Frances Jack at The Scotch Whisky Research Institute; Professor Barry Smith, University of London; Ian Weir, Ian Macleod Distillers; Rachel MacNeil, The Islay Malt Whisky Academy; Emily Harris, May Fox PR; Catherine Bourassa, Edrington; Tarita Mullings, Story PR; Isabel Graham-Yooll, Whisky.Auction; Joe Wilson, Whisky Auctioneer.

Thank you very much to Alison Starling for commissioning this book, which I was super eager to write, and to Jeannie Stanley for editing with insight, patience and understanding.

Islay in numbers

Ardbeg

Barley: KWS Sassy

Semi-lauter mash tun: 4.5-tonne capacity

1st water: 17,500 litres (3,900 gallons) at 64°C (147°F), with one rotation of the rake

2nd water: 8,100 litres (1,800 gallons) at 82°C (180°F), once 10,000 litres (2,200 gallons) of 1st water have drained

3rd (sparge): 17,500 litres (3,900 gallons) at 98°C (208°F)

12 Oregon pine washbacks: 23,500-litre (5,200-gallon) capacity

Mashing: 6 hours

12 Oregon pine washbacks: 23,500-litre (5,200-gallon) capacity

Mauri yeast

Fermentation time: 66 hours

1 wash still: 11,775-litre (2,590-gallon) capacity

1st distillation peak: 48–49% abv, decreasing to 1% abv, low wines around 25% abv

2nd distillation peak: 80% abv before decreasing

Foreshots: 10–15 minutes, aromatic, fruity, pear drops and floral notes, accompanied by some smoke

Spirit cut: 73–62.5% abv, with phenols coming over throughout; Heavier phenolics from 3 hours; ends after 4½ hours, representing 19% of the original charge.

New make spirit: 69% abv

Ardnahoe

Lauter mash tun with copper lid

1st water: 10,500 litres (2,300 gallons) at 64.5 °C (148°F)

2nd water: 3,300 litres (725 gallons) at 80°C (176°F), added once final drop of 1st water has drained

4 Oregon pine washbacks

Fermentation time: 70–75 hours

Wash still capacity: 12,500 litres (2,700 gallons)

Low wines: 25–26% abv

Spirit still capacity: 9,000 litres (2,000 gallons)

Heads: a few minutes

Spirit cut: 2–2½ hours

Feints: 3–3½ hours

New make spirit: strength not disclosed

Bowmore

Barley: Laureate

Semi-lauter mash tun with copper lid: 8-tonne capacity

1st water: 27,000 litres (6,000 gallons) at 63.5°C (146°F), accompanied by one ration of the arm

2nd water: 13,000 litres (2,900 gallons) at 85°C (185°F), added after half the 1st water drained

3rd water: 27,000 litres (6,000 gallons) at 100°C (212°F), added after most of 2nd water has drained (recycled as sparge, containing phenolics and residual sugars)

7 Oregon pine washbacks: 40,000-litre (8,800-gallon) capacity

Fermentation time: 62 hours

Wash still capacity: 2 stills at 20,000 litres (4,400 gallons) each; low wines with richer, earthier flavours and a strength of around 22% abv

Spirit still capacity: 2 stills at 23,500 litres (5,200 gallons) each

Foreshots: 20 minutes

Spirit cut: 74–61% abv, over 2–2½ hours

Feints: 3–3½ hours

Shell and tube condensers: each contains 264 three-metre (ten-feet) long tubes, 16 mm (½ in) diameter, spaced 10 mm (¼in) apart

Filling strength: 63.5% abv

Bunnahabhain

Barley: Laureate

Mash tun

1st water: 50,000 litres (1,100 gallons) at 63.8°C (147°F); if any stirring is required to help drainage, bed left to 'sit' for 10-15 minutes before water drained)

2nd water: 23,000 litres (5,100 gallons) at 80°C (176°F)

3rd water: 23,000 litres (5,100 gallons) at 90°C (194°F), once 2nd water has drained)

4th water: 20,000 litres (4,400 gallons) at 90°C (194°F)

3rd and 4th waters effectively continuous and combined as sparge

Mashing cycle: 10–12 hours

6 Oregon pine washbacks: 66,500-litre (15,000-gallon) capacity (dating from 1963, 1994 and 1995)

Fermentation time: 54 hours

Wash still capacity: 2 stills at 35,386 litres (7,800 gallons) each

Spirit still capacity: 2 stills at 15,546 litres (3,400 gallons) each

1st distillation: 5½ hours, producing low wines at 24–27% abv, to which the foreshots and feints of the previous distillation are added

2nd distillation: 7 hours, beginning with 10 minutes of foreshots

Spirit cut: begins at 74% abv and lasts about 2 hours

Unpeated spirit: spirit cut ends at 64% abv

Peated spirit: spirit cut ends at 61.5% abv

Filling strength: 69% abv

Bruichladdich

Rake mash tun: rarity, series of arms fitted with additional 'teeth'

1st water: 23,500 (5,100 gallons) litres at 64°C (147°F)

2nd water: 12,500 litres (2,700 gallons) at 85°C (185°F); first 2 waters provide the wort)

3rd water: 23,500 litres (5,200 gallons) at 88°C (190°F)

4th water: 12,500 litres (2,700 gallons) at 93°C (200°F); these last 2 waters form the sparge)

6 Oregon pine washbacks: 45,000-litre (9,900-gallon) capacity

Fermentation time: 72 hours (week), 100 hours (weekend) – washes distilled separately, but blended prior to filling casks

2 wash stills: 17,500-litre (3,800-gallon) capacity each, and steam-heated

1st distillation: 5–6 hours, 24–25% abv, showing fruit, but Bruichladdich has more pears and apples than Octomore, which is oilier and thicker

2nd distillation: peaks around 74–75% abv

Foreshots: collected down to 73% abv, which takes around 35 minutes, characterized by nail varnish, earthy, oily notes

Spirit cut: begins at 73% abv with burst of fruit, vanilla, cereal and biscuit notes appearing together, then individual sequence begins with dried apple skin, dried pear skin; continues to 63% abv, then goes to tails just before the spirit emits smell of sweaty trainers and stale water

Feints: 4 hours, around 28–29% abv

Filling strength: 69% abv

Caol Ila

Lauter mash tun

1st water: 49,000 litres (11,000 gallons) at 64°C (147°F)

Approximately 50,500 litres (11,100 gallons) of water added continuously, temperature rising from 70°C (158°F) to 85°C (185°F)

8 Oregon pine washbacks: 53,000-litre (11,700-gallon) capacity

2 stainless steel washbacks: 51,000-litre (11,200-gallon) capacity

Fermentation time: 60 hours

Wash stills: 3 stills are charged with 17,000–17,500 litres (3,700–3,800 gallons)

Spirit stills: 3 stills at 11,000 litres (2,400 gallons)

1st distillation: 4–6 hours, producing low wines at 24–26% abv with distinct apple notes and phenolics

2nd distillation: 6 hours, beginning with 20 minutes of foreshots

Spirit cut: 75% abv–64% abv; this represents about 25 per cent of the total charge, with a peating level around 10–15 ppm (compared to malted barley at 38–40 ppm)

Distillation strength: 70% abv

Kilchoman

Barley: Sassy and Publican

Semi-lauter mash tun: 1.2-tonne capacity (each water stirred once, 'infused' slowly for 30 minutes, then drained slowly to obtain clear wort)

1st water: 19,000 litres (4,200 gallons) at 64°C (147°F)

2nd water: 22,000 litres (4,800 gallons) at 70°C (158°F); once 5,000 litres (1,100 gallons) of 1st water have drained

3rd water: 19,000 litres (4,200 gallons) at 84°C (183°F)

14 stainless steel washbacks: 6,000-litre (1,300-gallon) capacity each

Fermentation time: 85 hours

2 wash stills

1st distillation: peaks at around 40% abv, then decreases; low wines are 20–25% abv, to which the heads and tails are added

2nd distillation: peaks at around 76% abv, with 5 minutes of foreshots

New make spirit: collected from 75% abv for 90 minutes, down to 65.5% abv; the profile is fresh, floral and fruity, with the air in the stillhouse fragrant with pear drops, the character gradually becoming oilier, with smoke rather than peat evident later in the run

Filling strength: 63.5%

Lagavulin

1st water: 19,000 litres (4,200 gallons) at 64°C (147°F)

2nd water: 22,000 litres (4,800 gallons) at 70°C (148°F); once 5,000 litres of 1st water has drained)

3rd water: 19,000 litres (4,200 gallons) at 84°C (183°F)

Mashing: 5½ hours, 28–30 mashes a week

10 wooden washbacks, American larch: 22,000-litre (4,800-gallon) capacity

Fermentation time: 55 hours

Wash still capacity: 2 stills at 20,000 litres (4,400 gallons) each; low wines with richer, earthier flavours and a strength of around 22% abv

Spirit still capacity: 2 stills at 23,500 litres (5,200 gallons) each

Foreshots: 20 minutes

Spirit cut: 74–61% abv, over 2–2½ hours

Feints: 3–3½ hours

Shell and tube condensers: each contains 264 three-metre (10-feet) long tubes, 16 mm (½ in) diameter, spaced 10 mm (¼in) apart

Filling strength: 63.5% abv

Laphroaig

Lauter mash tun: 5.5-tonne capacity

1st water: 24,500 litres (5,400 gallons) at 63.5°C (146°F)

2nd & 3rd waters: total 53,500 litres (11,800 gallons) at 85 °C (185°F); added when 1st water has almost entirely drained)

Fermentation time: 72 hours

3 wash stills: 10,500-litre (2,300-gallon) capacity each

Low wines: 25% abv in 6½ hours, creating fruitiness and maximizing phenolics

Spirit stills: 3 with 4,700-litre (1000-gallon) capacity and boil bowls to increase reflux; 1 with 9,400-litre (2,100-gallon) capacity

Foreshots: 45 minutes

Spirit cut: 72–c.60% abv, 2¼ hours 15 minutes

New make spirit: 68% abv

Filling strength: 63.5% abv

Index

About the author

Ian Wisniewski is a food, drink
and travel writer and broadcaster,
specializing in spirits, particularly Scotch
whisky. He is the author of five books on
whisky, including *The Whisky Dictionary*
and *Classic Malt Whisky*, and has written
for various publications including
Whisky Magazine and *Malt Whisky
Yearbook*, while also contributing to
Michael Jackson's encyclopaedic
book, *Whisky*. He has presented at the
Worldwide Distilled Spirits Conference
and Craft Expo, conducts tutored
tastings and classes on whisky, is a
judge for various competitions including
the Speyside Whisky Festival, and
regularly visits distilleries to keep
learning more about the production
process, one of his favourite subjects.
He is a Master of the Quaich, the highest
honour bestowed by the Keepers of the
Quaich, an international organisation
that recognizes commitment and
contributions to Scotch whisky.

First published in Great Britain in 2023
by Mitchell Beazley, an imprint of
Octopus Publishing Group Ltd
Carmelite House
50 Victoria Embankment
London EC4Y 0DZ
www.octopusbooks.co.uk
www.octopusbooksusa.com

An Hachette UK Company
www.hachette.co.uk

Text copyright © Ian Wisniewski 2023
Illustrations copyright © Melvyn Evans 2023
Design and layout copyright © Octopus
Publishing Group 2023

Distributed in the US by
Hachette Book Group
1290 Avenue of the Americas
4th and 5th Floors
New York, NY 10104

Distributed in Canada by
Canadian Manda Group
664 Annette St.
Toronto, Ontario, Canada M6S 2C8

ISBN 978-1-78472-909-7

A CIP catalogue record for this book is
available from the British library.

Printed and bound in China.

10 9 8 7 6 5 4 3 2 1

Publisher: Alison Starling
Junior Editor: Jeannie Stanley
Editorial Assistant: Ellen Sleath
Art Director: Jonathan Christie
Copy-Editor: Laura Gladwin
Proofreader: Jo Richardson
Senior Production Manager: Peter Hunt

MIX
Paper | Supporting
responsible forestry
FSC® C008047